Business Process Automation

Springer

Berlin
Heidelberg
New York
Hong Kong
London
Milan
Paris
Tokyo

August-Wilhelm Scheer
Ferri Abolhassan
Wolfram Jost
Mathias Kirchmer
Editors

Business Process Automation

ARIS in Practice

With 72 Figures
and 6 Tables

  Springer

Professor Dr. Dr. h.c. mult. August-Wilhelm Scheer
Founder and Chairman of the Supervisory Board
aw.scheer@ids-scheer.de

Dr. Ferri Abolhassan
Co-Chairman and CEO
f.abolhassan@ids-scheer.de

Dr. Wolfram Jost
Member of the Executive Board
w.jost@ids-scheer.de

IDS Scheer AG
Postfach 10 15 34, D-66015 Saarbruecken, Germany

Dr. Mathias Kirchmer
President and CEO, IDS Scheer, Inc, USA
Member of the extended Executive Board
IDS Scheer AG
1205 Westlakes Dr. Suite 270, Berwyn, PA 19312, USA
m.kirchmer@ids-scheer.com

ISBN 3-540-20794-5 Springer-Verlag Berlin Heidelberg New York

Cataloging-in-Publication Data applied for

A catalog record for this book is available from the Library of Congress.

Bibliographic information published by Die Deutsche Bibliothek
Die Deutsche Bibliothek lists this publication in the Deutsche Nationalbibliografie;
detailed bibliographic data available in the internet at *http.//dnb.ddb.de*

Springer-Verlag is a part of Springer Science+Business Media
springeronline.com

© Springer-Verlag Heidelberg 2004
Printed in Germany

Cover design: Erich Kirchner, Heidelberg

SPIN 10980415   42/3130 – 5 4 3 2 1 0 – Printed on acid-free paper

Foreword

Enterprises have to adapt their business processes quickly and efficiently to new business environments to ensure business success and long-term survival. It is not sufficient to apply best business practices as it is also necessary to develop and execute new practices. These requirements are met by new business process automation technologies, based on concepts such as web services, EAI, workflow, component-based software, enterprise service architectures and automation engines. Business process automation becomes a key enabler for business process excellence.

This book explains major trends in business process automation and shows how new technologies and solutions are applied in practice. It outlines how process automation becomes an element of an overall process lifecycle management approach, structured with the ARIS House of Business Process Excellence as a basis and implemented through software tools such as the ARIS Process Platform.

This is the third volume of the "ARIS in Practice" book series. The first volume, entitled "Business Process Excellence", showed – using multiple case studies – how enterprises approach business process lifecycle management applying solutions based on the ARIS framework. "Business Process Change Management", the second volume, highlighted the people side of process management. This new volume, "Business Process Automation", focuses on the technology aspects of process lifecycle management and how process automation technologies are used in a business-driven way in order to achieve competitive advantages.

We would like to thank all those authors who contributed to this book. Their willingness to share their knowledge and experiences will help many other organizations. Thanks also to the entire team who supported this book project from an administrative point of view.

Berwyn, USA
Saarbrücken, Germany
January 2004

Prof. Dr. Dr. h.c. mult. August-Wilhelm Scheer   Dr. Ferri Abolhassan

Dr. Wolfram Jost   Dr. Mathias Kirchmer

Table of Contents

Peter Westermann, DC Bank AG
Frank Gahse, IDS Scheer AG

Colin Western, Major Hollywood Motion Picture Studio
Emmanuel Hadzipetros, IDS Scheer, Inc.

Rajiv Lajmi, IDS Scheer SME Midatlantic
Jeff Michaels, IDS Scheer SME Midatlantic
Chris Snyder, IDS Scheer SME Midatlantic

Thomas R. Gulledge, George Mason University
Greg Huntington, Enterprise Integration, Inc.
Wael Hafez, IDS Scheer, Inc.
Georg Simon, IDS Scheer, Inc.

Otmar Adam, Institute of Information Systems, Universität des Saarlandes
Dirk Werth, Institute of Information Systems, Universität des Saarlandes
Fabrice Zangl, Institute of Information Systems, Universität des Saarlandes

Business Process Automation – Combining Best and Next Practices

Mathias Kirchmer
IDS Scheer North America and Japan
Center for Organizational Dynamics, University of Pennsylvania, USA

August-Wilhelm Scheer
IDS Scheer AG
Institute of Information Systems (IWi), Universität des Saarlandes, Germany

Summary

In order to achieve constant growth and survive long term, enterprises have to innovate continuously. They therefore have to combine best and next business practices. Best practices ensure efficiency; next practices really lead to competitive advantages.

Traditional business process automation solutions such as ERP, SCM or CRM systems focus on the implementation of best practices. Next-generation process automation allows the implementation of next practices at an economically acceptable cost level. This is possible through a flexible combination of business process definition and software application support. The appropriate software support is dynamically configured with the business processes definition as a basis so that it enables the execution of enterprise-specific processes.

Business process models reflecting best and next practices drive the configuration of next-generation process automation solutions. They become the critical link between strategy and execution.

Key Words

ARIS, ARIS Toolset, ARIS House of Business Process Excellence, Business Process Automation, Business Process Management, Composite Applications, EAI, Enterprise Service Architecture, Outsourcing, Real-Time Enterprise, Reference Models, Web Services

1   Business Success Through Best and Next Practices

In order to achieve stable growth and survive long term, enterprises have to innovate continuously. It is not sufficient just to implement best business practices or to reduce costs. In general, best practices only ensure the consolidation of an existing business and market position. Real progress is made through innovation. And innovation requires the development and execution of next business practices, reflected in new processes. Successful enterprises have to combine best and next practices to achieve business process excellence, which in turn leads to competitive advantages [cf. Scheer 2003].

1.1 Innovation Drives Next Practices

An enterprise can drive innovation in various ways. The key types of innovation are:

- Product innovation

- Collaboration innovation

- Process innovation

These types of innovation are interrelated. They all influence each other. Product innovation may also imply collaboration and process innovation and so on. The types of innovation and their interrelations are visualized in figure 1: Types of innovation.

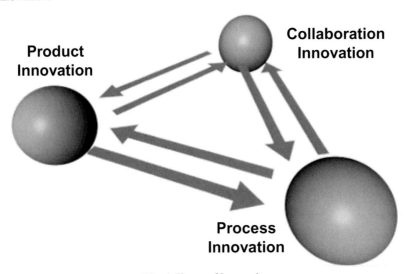

Fig. 1. Types of Innovation

The classic form of innovation is product innovation. The term "product" is used here in a broad sense which includes goods, services, rights or any other offering sold on the market [cf. Kirchmer 1999, Market-...]. Product innovation means that a new product is brought onto the market or the features of an existing one are multiplied or improved. A new digital camera may have a better resolution and an easier integration with a PC, a car an advanced board computer, or a consulting company offers a new service solution focused on the Sarbanes-Oxley act.

"Collaboration Innovation" has become more and more important. New forms of collaboration result in competitive advantages, e.g. new offerings. An example of this type of innovation are the "On Star" services, which GM first offered in the Cadillac Escalade. Through On Star, the driver can connect to a service office. There they locate the car, give directions or offer concierge services. The car itself was not really an innovation when it appeared on the market, but the combination with On Star was. This innovation was possible through a unique collaboration between a car company and a wireless network phone company. The collaborative innovation resulted in an enhanced offering, a product innovation.

The third type of innovation is process innovation. In this case, innovation is driven through new or uniquely improved business processes. Companies like Dell, Amazon.com or Ebay are built entirely on the basis of process innovation. Dell didn't invent the PC, but a new process of introducing it on the market; Amazon did not invent the book but a new way of selling it; and Ebay offers a new, unique way of participating in auctions. In these cases, new processes lead to new ways of collaborating and new offerings.

In general, each type of innovation has an impact on the business processes on the spot. This is obvious in the case of process innovation. But a new form of collaboration also requires new processes appropriate to it, in this case inter-enterprise processes. And new or modified products that have to be produced and sold may result in new sales, production or distribution processes. These innovation-driven processes are in most cases unique when they are first implemented. They therefore require next business practices. Best practices are not available for these business processes.

1.2 Efficiency Drives Best Practices

However, the innovation does not require new processes – next practices – in all areas of an enterprise. On the contrary: Many consulting research projects have shown that 80% or more of a company's business processes can often be standardized with industry best practices as a basis without any impact on the desired competitive advantages of an organization. This reduces costs and risk for the implementation and management of these processes [cf. Kirchmer et al. 2002] [cf. Kirchmer 1999, Business...].

Typical examples of the use of such best practices are processes that are highly influenced by legal regulations, e.g. in the field of finance, accounting or human resources administration. In general, it wouldn't make sense to invent new processes in these areas. However, the implementation of best-practice business processes can also make sense in areas that are widely recognized as important for creating competitive advantages. The distribution processes of a supply chain may be crucial and unique for some packaged pharmaceutical or consumer goods companies. They may be less relevant for an enterprise in the capital goods industries. Here the use of best practices is the most efficient solution.

Industry organizations such as the Supply Chain Council develop best practice reference models that allow the efficient and effective use of such business process standards. An example of such a reference model is shown in figure 2: SCOR reference model – best practice model for the supply chain. The SCOR reference model structures the supply chain processes on higher levels based on best practices, and on the lowest description level leaves the appropriate choice of a company-specific execution of those processes, including the implementation of new processes.

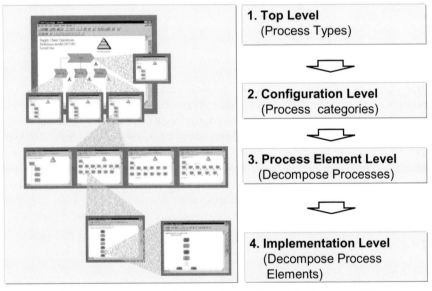

Fig. 2. SCOR Reference Model – Best Practice Model for the Supply Chain

The systematic use of such best-practice models is the key for an organization to efficiently reach the necessary process improvements in areas where they do not need to achieve special competitive advantages. Here, a company has to be at least as good as the competition, and this with as little effort as possible. To try to define next practices in these areas would lead to unnecessary costs and therefore even have a negative impact on the business situation of an enterprise. The efficient and effective application of best practices itself often becomes an important competitive advantage for an organization.

2   Business Process Automation – the Key Enabler

Best business and next business practices have to be identified, combined and then effectively implemented in the organization. This requires a systematic approach to business process lifecycle management. A framework that enables such an approach is the ARIS House of Business Process Excellence. It ensures the design, implementation, execution and control of business processes based on best and next practices.

Ultimately, however, the desired business results can be fully achieved only if the execution of the processes is successful. Widely used standard application software solutions such as ERP, SCM or CRM systems support the execution of processes but generally lead to the realization of best-practice scenarios. The implementation of next practices requires flexibility in execution that, up to now, has not been available or only at an unacceptable price. As a result, many processes are not or not sufficiently automated [cf. Kalakota & Robinson 2003]. The results are reduced performance and productivity. The use of new business process automation technologies therefore becomes crucial: they deliver the necessary flexibility when executing the process to implement new business-process practices at an acceptable cost level.

2.1 Business Process Lifecycle Management

The entire lifecycle of business processes can be managed with the ARIS House of Business Process Excellence shown in figure 3 as a basis: ARIS House of Business Process Excellence [cf. Jost & Scheer 2002] [cf. Kirchmer & Scheer 2003], leading to a process-centered organization. An enterprise organized in this way can adapt quickly to changing business environments ("adaptive enterprise"), triggered through events such as new or changing customer, supplier or other market partner requirements, new or modified market offerings, changing legal regulations, availability of new or improved technologies, outsourcing of specific activities, mergers and acquisitions, new business models, or cultural differences in various locations. Business-process-based organizations are able to fulfill short-term needs and maintain long-term success.

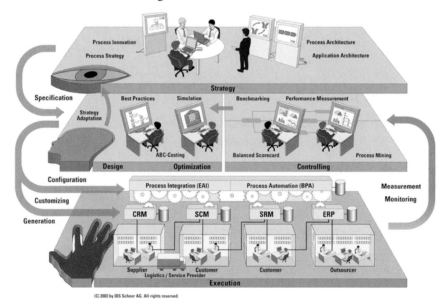

Fig. 3. Three-Tier Architecture of Business Process Excellence

Business process management starts on the strategy level of an organization. Here, the planned innovation is identified and the resulting business process structure and strategy as well as the business goals are defined. Those processes requiring next business practices in order to lead to competitive advantages are identified. The underlying application system architecture is then worked out accordingly. The guideline for a process-centered organization is laid out.

This guideline is passed from the strategy level to the process specification level. On this level, the blueprint for the resulting business processes is specified, using techniques such as simulation or ABC costing. Processes reflecting next practices are designed from scratch. Specification of processes based on best practices can be supported using the above-mentioned reference models. On the specification level, all the necessary business processes are described in detail so that this description can be used to drive the execution of the process. The result is a blueprint consisting of business-process models.

Based on these process models, all physical and information-processing activities are implemented within and across enterprises. Here, either processes are executed using standard application packages such as ERP, SCM or CRM systems which more or less support best practice processes, or processes must be executed with more flexible application solutions that can reflect necessary next practice approaches as a basis. These are next-generation business process automation solutions.

The processes actually executed are measured and controlled on the so-called controlling level. If differences are observed between planned key performance indicators (KPIs), defined with the goals identified on the strategy level as a basis, and the actual values, either a continuous improvement process is initiated through the process specification layer or the situation is resolved on a strategic level if the business environment has changed significantly.

All design, specification and controlling activities can be supported by business process management solutions such as the ARIS Process Platform [cf. IDS Scheer AG (Ed.) 2003]. These solutions also drive the process execution, that may be based on traditional process automation or next-generation process automation solutions.

2.2 Traditional Process Automation

During the last ten to fifteen years, more and more business processes have been supported by standard software packages such as ERP, SCM, or CRM systems [cf. Kirchmer 1999, Business...]. This has numerous advantages over individually developed software systems. A key advantage of these traditional process automation solutions is that they do more than deliver a technology to execute a specific process. Standard software also supplies best business practices, included in the software.

Successful use of standard software such as ERP systems also implies the definition and execution of business processes according to the software solution. Standard software systems include a process definition that is more or less coded in the software. This allows no or only minor changes to the process definition. Modifications to the process logic result in software modifications that lead to tremendous costs.

Those process definitions delivered through standard software are increasingly described in so-called software reference models. These software reference models document the best practices supported by the application system. Next business practices are generally not supported. The reason for this is that they require new processes that no one had in mind during the standard software development. Only when, in the course of time, a next practice becomes a best practice will it be included in the traditional software solution. The fixed integration of process definition and software technology in traditional standard software systems is visualized in figure 4: Traditional standard software: Fixed integration of process definition and software.

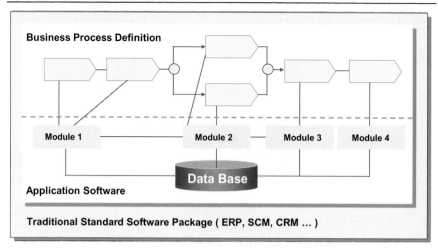

Fig. 4. Traditional Standard Software: Fixed Integration of Process Definition and Software

While application software systems such as SAP's mySAP, for example, allow the customizing of thousands of tables to influence the process logic – resulting in alternatives in reference models – they still only reflect various best practices. If you do not want to follow the project logic of an ERP or other standard software system, this generally causes huge challenges which can only be resolved through major software development investments, not only for the development of add-ons but also for their integration and maintenance. This leads to dramatically increased total ownership costs. As a result, new business processes used are not to be supported by traditional software solutions, which have a negative impact on productivity and performance.

Next business practices therefore have to be supported by new software architectures – by next-generation process automation – which ensure the necessary flexibility, combined with acceptable costs.

2.3 Next-Generation Process Automation

The basis for next-generation business process automation is the separation of the application software itself, the integration technologies and the business process design. The application software provides the functionality needed to support a business process. The integration technologies, often called business process automation engines, consist logically of a workflow component that enforces the necessary process logic and a data-integration component, so-called enterprise application integration (EAI), that ensures the availability of the required data. This structure is shown in figure 5: Components of next-generation process automation: Process definition, integration, and application.

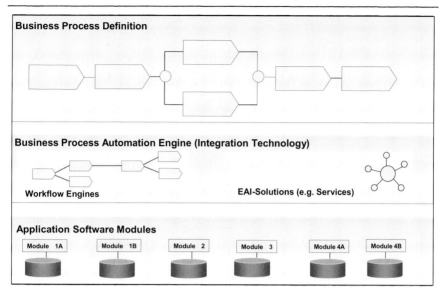

Fig. 5. Components of Next-Generation Process Automation: Process Definition, Integration, Application

New business processes are defined in process models, representing the process definition. These models are detailed until they are specific enough, so that the workflow engine can be configured more or less automatically based on those models. This is possible through the use of standards for developing the most specifric level of process models, such as the business process modeling language "BPML" [cf. BPMI (Ed.) 2003, Business Process Modeling Language...][cf. BPMI (Ed.) 2003, Business Process Modeling Notation...] or the business process execution language "BPEL" [cf. Thatte 2003]. These standards ensure that the workflow engine "understands" the process definition.

The workflow engine then "organizes" when and which application functionality is needed and activates it accordingly. The EAI environment ensures the availability of the necessary data, which is transformed into a neutral format so that it can be forwarded from one application to the next as required through the process definition. This procedure is visualized in figure 6: Next-generation process automation: How it works.

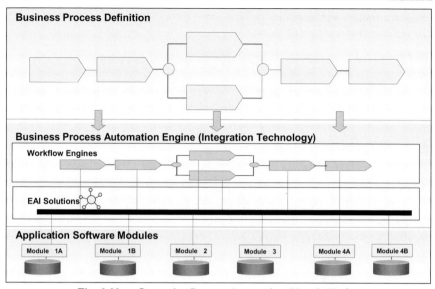

Fig. 6. Next-Generation Process Automation: How it Works

Next-generation business process automation is technically implemented with new software architectures as a basis. Existing applications may be split or combined in order to deliver the appropriate functionality needed in various processes. The application functionality combined with the data involved and the logical procedure of applying the functionality to the data is often called a "component". Such a component delivers a "service" that can then be used by another component according to the defined business process logic. This allows integration of applications without using difficult means to maintain interfaces. If such a service is offered through the Internet using specific standardized protocols, it is called a "web service". IT architectures that support such a flexible next-generation business process automation are called Enterprise Service Architectures [cf. Kalakota & Robinson 2003][cf. Woods 2003].

These next-generation process automation environments deliver the flexibility necessary for supporting next business practices at an acceptable cost level. Existing application software is used as far as possible; only really non-existent functionality has to be developed. No specific interfaces are to be developed or maintained, which again reduces the total cost of ownership [cf. Woods 2003][cf. Bruckert & Grasman 2003].

Next-generation process automation solutions can be used to support processes within an enterprise or across various enterprises. They therefore enable intra- and inter-enterprise processes.

However, such automation solutions require a very thorough process definition. The development of appropriate business process models is the key for the successful use of such process automation solutions and, in turn, for the execution of the defined process strategy as well.

SAP's NetWeaver is an example of an IT environment that supports such a next-generation process automation [cf. Bruckert & Haendly 2003]. Microsoft, IBM, Oracle, BEA and numerous smaller vendors create and deliver similar solutions [cf. Schulte 2003].

2.4 Composite Applications

As explained, this new generation of process automation allows existing applications to be combined with new applications seamlessly, avoiding integration challenges known from traditional application environments. This allows the integration of best and next practices.

However, in order to automize next-practice business processes, you may not even need new, non-existing application functionality. It may be sufficient to use existing application functionality in a new process logic. Next-generation process automation environments provide for rapid development of such "composite applications". They deliver a process definition, an appropriately configured workflow and data integration, and use one or several existing software modules. Composite applications support a specific "new" business process which has not been supported by the existing standard software solution. They represent the business content of next-generation process automation systems.

These composite applications may be created with previously implemented standard software packages such as ERP, SCM or CRM systems [cf. Woods 2003] as a basis, allowing an enterprise to use these systems in a new way. These composite applications may also add the functionality of available specialized third-party software in order to support the defined business process. The idea of these composite applications is visualized in figure 7: Composite applications: New processes based on existing applications.

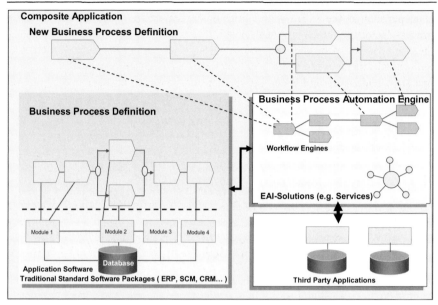

Fig. 7. Composite Applications: New Processes Based on Existing Applications

These composite applications, built on existing standard software, can be offered on the market as packaged solutions – a way of distributing next business practices [cf. Woods 2003]. Software or consulting companies or even end-use companies may develop such composite applications and offer them as "next practices". These next practices will then, step by step, become best practices.

Examples of packaged composite applications are SAP xApps [cf. Stolz 2003] that are offered by SAP and partners and provide new process solutions based on existing SAP applications.

3   The Business Process Factory – a Critical Link

The key to efficient and effective use of these next-generation process automation solutions is the structured and reusable definition of the business processes to be supported. These business processes reflect the combination of best and next practices. These processes are defined in process models on the specification level of the ARIS House of Business Process Excellence, described above [cf. Scheer 1998, Business Process Frameworks…] [cf. Scheer 1998, Business Process Modeling…].

As explained above, these models are the key to successful use of next-generation process automation environments. They have to be developed and modified frequently in order to support continuous innovation and improvement reflected in concepts such as the adaptive enterprise or the real-time enterprise. The business process factory is the environment enabling the productivity and performance of the management of business process models [cf. Kirchmer et al. 2002]. It forms the critical link between the strategic decision to innovate and improve and the operative realization and execution of that decision. The concept of the process factory is shown in figure 8: Business process factory – efficient and effective.

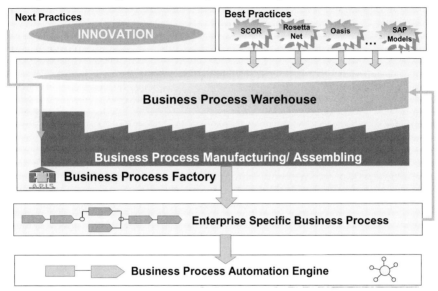

Fig. 8. Business Process Factory – Efficient and Effective

Best practices are available on the market in the form of process reference models. They are delivered by industry organizations such as the Supply Chain Council, RossettaNet, BPMI or Oasis, by consulting companies or by software companies [cf. Kirchmer 1999, Business…]. These models are stored in a database called the "business process warehouse". They can be used as "best-practice process components" for specifying enterprise-specific business processes.

In the process manufacturing and assembling unit, enterprise-specific business process models are either "assembled" using those process components available, or new processes are manufactured with the planned innovations of an enterprise as a basis. The result is the desired combination of best and next practices, reflected in the enterprise-specific process models.

These enterprise-specific models have to be consistent and accurately reflect the desired future business processes. Every mistake in the process models leads to a mistake in the ensuing execution. For this reason, the simulation of processes, the development and comparison of various scenarios and a thorough cost and time analysis of the designed processes are extremely important and a core component of the assembling and manufacturing process.

These process models are forwarded to the next-generation process automation environment, where they drive the configuration of the workflow and integration solution. This ensures that the process is executed according to the developed process design.

The process models are also stored in the process warehouse. This allows for subsequent reuse for a rollout to other locations, mergers & acquisitions, or just a further improvement of the process.

This process factory can be physically materialized using e.g. the ARIS Business Process Platform [cf. IDS Scheer AG (Ed.) 2003] – as part of the overall process lifecycle management – explained above. The integration of the ARIS solutions into process automation environments such as SAP's NetWeaver or solutions form vendors such as WebV2, Intalio, Savvion or Vitiria, for example, allows the seamless handover of the process models and their reuse in the automation environments to drive the configuration.

The business process factory enables the efficient business-driven use of next-generation process environments to achieve competitive advantages. Technology enablers are environments such as the ARIS business process platform.

4   References

BPMI (Ed.): Business Process Modeling Language – BPML 1.0 Specification 2003. In: BPMI.org

BPMI (Ed.): Business Process Modeling Notation – BPMN 1.0 Specification 2003. In: BPMI.org

Bruckert, S., Grasman, D.: The Benefits of SAP Net Weaver. In: SAP AG (Ed.): SAP Info – Quick Guide: SAP NetWeaver – The Power of Lower TCO, 4/2003, p. 8-9.

Bruckert, S., Haendly, M.: SAP NetWeaver key capabilities – At a Glance. In: SAP AG (Ed.): SAP Info – Quick Guide: SAP NetWeaver – The Power of Lower TCO, 4/2003, p. 10-11.

Elzina, D.J., Gulledge, T.R., Lee, C.-Y. (Ed.): Business Engineering. Norwell 1999.

IDS Scheer AG (Ed.): The ARIS Process Platform. In: ids-scheer.com, 11/2003.

Jost, W., Scheer, A.-W.: Business Process Management: A Core Task for any Company Organization. In: Scheer, A.-W., Abolhassan, F., Jost, W., Kirchmer, M.: Business Process Excellence – ARIS in Practice. Berlin, New York, and others 2002, p. 33-43.

Kalakota, R., Robinson, M.: Service Blueprints – Roadmap for Execution. Boston, New York, and others 2003.

Kirchmer, M., Brown, G., Heinzel, H.: Using SCOR and Other Reference Models for E-Business Process Networks. In: Scheer, A.-W., Abolhassan, F., Jost, W., Kirchmer, M. (ed.): Business Process Excellence – ARIS in Practice. Berlin, New York, and others 2002, p. 45-64.

Kirchmer, M., Scheer, A.-W.: Change Management – Key for Business Process Excellence. In: Scheer, A.-W., Abolhassan, F., Jost, W., Kirchmer, M. (ed.): Business Process Change Management – ARIS in Practice. Berlin, New York, and others 2003, p. 1-14.

Kirchmer, M.: Business Process Oriented Implementation of Standard Software – How to Achieve Competitive Advantage Efficiently and Effectively. 2nd edition, Berlin, New York and others 1999.

Kirchmer, M.: Market- and Product-Oriented Definition of Business Processes. In: Elzina, D.J., Gulledge, T.R., Lee, C.-Y. (Ed.): Business Engineering. Norwell 1999, p. 131-144.

Scheer, A.-W., Abolhassan, F., Jost, W., Kirchmer, M. (ed.): Business Process Excellence – ARIS in Practice. Berlin, New York, and others 2002.

Scheer, A.-W., Abolhassan, F., Jost, W., Kirchmer, M. (ed.): Business Process Change Management – ARIS in Practice. Berlin, New York, and others 2003.

Scheer, A.-W.: ARIS – Business Process Frameworks. 2nd edition, Berlin, New York and others 1998.

Scheer, A.-W.: ARIS – Business Process Modeling. 2nd edition, Berlin, New York and others 1998.

Scheer, A.-W.: Business Process Engineering – The New Wave? In: IDS Scheer, Inc. (Ed.): Proceedings of ProcessWorld 2003. Philadelphia 2003.

Schulte, R.: Application Integration. In: Gartner Group (Ed.): Client issues for application integration, 11/06/2003.

Stolz, H.: Composite Applications Framework – Designing Cross Solutions. In: SAP AG (Ed.): SAP Info – Quick Guide: SAP NetWeaver – The Power of Lower TCO, 4/2003, p. 40.

Thatte, S. (Ed.): Business Process Execution Language for Web Services [BPEL4WS] 05/05/2003. In: XML.coverpages.org

Woods, D.: Packaged Composite Applications. Beijing, Cambridge, Cologne, and others 2003.

Woods, Dan: Enterprise Service Architectures. Beijing, Cambridge, Cologne, and others 2003.

Process Automation Using the Real-Time Enterprise Concept

Ferri Abolhassan
IDS Scheer AG

Björn Welchering
IDS Scheer AG

Summary

There are many facets to Business Process Automation. Alongside system automation through EAI, SAP Netweaver or classic ERP, CRM and SCM systems, today there is also the Real-Time Enterprise (RTE) concept, which has developed into a megatrend for businesses.

Time and again, however, isolated new IT solutions or strategic concepts obscure the view of the fundamental holistic approach of RTE. This presentation is intended to provide an overview of the potentials of, and of the demands placed upon, an RTE, and to explain how Business Process Automation provides the basics for RTE. Various examples will be used to illustrate possible processes of, and the use of, RTE.

The purpose of this article is to illustrate an understanding of the customer's desire for processing speed and quality as the source of the RTE approach, extending to process optimization and implementation of systems as the infrastructural basis of the real-time enterprise. We want to make clear that the automation of business processes, technology, strategy and management in businesses, particularly in the RTE, cannot exist independently of one another.

Key Words

Real-Time Enterprise, Business Process Automation, Lead Times, Strategy, Management, ARIS Process Platform, SAP Netweaver

1   Introduction

The previous chapter dealt with both the significance of Business Process Automation and the savings potentials which this involves. Thus, in its individual
shapes and sizes, Business Process Automation can either remain tied to traditional IT applications – as for example in isolated systems such as ERP, SCM or
CRM applications - or else it can be achieved through technological solutions in
the EAI or Web-services area.

In this connection, Business Process Automation can achieve cost reductions,
thereby helping achieve a strategic dimension of cost leadership; it can also provide support to a service component within the business itself. In the text which
follows, we describe how Business Process Automation and the Real-Time Enterprise concept help enable an enterprise to act more successfully in the marketplace
over the long term, together with the fundamental conditions which must be created in order for this to take place.

2   The RTE Concept

"The customer is king." The rise of the Internet during the 1990's, however, has
meant a drastic transformation in the demands made upon businesses' speed and
flexibility. As a result, increasingly autonomous consumers are turning to the
World Wide Web to make their own direct comparisons of price and delivery
times, taking their business to the most agile provider – only to abandon them very
shortly thereafter the moment companies can no longer perform the services
promised. This is compounded by the fact that market trends spread and morph
within days – not in locally circumscribed sales areas but worldwide. To survive, a
company needs to be quick and flexible. The factor of time is becoming the decisive distinguishing factor. Market trends need to be identified in real time, with all
of a company's resources mobilized and available without delay. This is the only
way to safeguard customer satisfaction, and the only way of ensuring sales of a
company's products into the future. Given the way in which many companies are
organized today, however, this mission can no longer be fulfilled.

Yet how can an intermeshing of activities within a company be achieved in real
time? Business Process Automation is an essential step towards success here. Still,
it is only one among many steps which must be taken.

To this day, at all levels of decision-making and activity, for the most part managers and staff are generally forced to work with historical information. Naturally,
the result of this is that a company can react only in delayed fashion to changed
customer behavior or shifting market conditions; this turns the factor of time into a
profit killer.

The Real-Time Enterprise concept, which the Gartner Group, an American market-research company, proclaimed a megatrend and must for companies in November 2002 at its Symposium/Itxpo in Cannes, France, is a logical consequence
of the technological progress made in the last few years, progress which spawned
a high degree of interconnection and integration. In other words, it is technological
developments which have made today's real-time economy possible.

For Gartner, too, the foundations for this sweeping statement are the far-reaching
changes which have come about as a result of the Internet and "new economy".
These have led to a "now economy" in which patience is no longer a virtue. The
claims made by Gartner are clear and unmistakable: the modern RTE must begin
by truncating all of its process times. Thus, in principle, there is no plausible reason why, in a make-to-stock environment, the delivery of an article cannot follow
immediately once an order has been placed – if only the process has been per-
fected. What counts are results: the merchandise must reach its destination as
quickly as possible. Intermediate steps are no longer tolerable.

Gartner also makes clear what the demands on information technology are in
terms of the processes involved: delays in application systems and interruptions of
processes must be measured, registered, analyzed and eliminated. The business architecture of the future must be designed to support processes in optimum fashion,
and free of delay. To this end, in Gartner's view, the following technological preconditions must be satisfied:

- An architecture must work without delays in order to support a shortening in
  process times

- Mobile and wireless technologies are needed so that the processes can be ad-
  justed at will in terms of both space and time

- In order to incorporate the entire company and, in the longer term, the entire
  value-added chain, the seamless integration of systems and creation of standards for data exchange is imperative

- Increases in service levels must proceed in tandem with enlistment of service-
  oriented IT architectures

Nonetheless, the Gartner Group does not envision a focus on the introduction of
new technologies – instead, most of what companies need is already in place, yet
far from comprehensively used.

Along with questions of IT - for which Gartner has drawn up clear guidelines -
there is, above all, the task of putting one's complete organization in a real-time
frame of mind - from production to sales and marketing, right up to the management level. This will make the future management of businesses practically impossible in the absence of real-time information: the successful navigation of an
enterprise calls for a great measure of farsightedness. Just as a captain who acts
responsibly does not rely solely on the water beneath his keel and the wind in his
sails, but also orients his decision-making around prevailing weather conditions

along the route ahead; so, too, is it indispensable for the manager to look beyond the company's own business processes.

This makes clear that the customer always and exclusively determines the origin and terminus of the holistic process chain. Fulfilling the customer's wishes must become a company's central task. In the final analysis, even B2B dealings are generated by consumer demand.

Since fundamental data such as market-research findings are made available not just to the marketing division but, automatically, to the development division as well, the development process for new products can be optimized quickly. In this connection, the term "time to market" comes automatically to mind as a significant performance gauge. Which is why service companies will also evolve into RTE. Thus, the factory principle, when tailored to banks, consulting firms and software manufacturers, is a possible step to take to react to the demands of the Real-Time Enterprise. Customer service, particularly in the services area, is considered a key opportunity for distinction. Under the RTE approach, this component can be developed accordingly to promote a sustained increase in a company's value.

The fundamentals of the process side of the RTE are to be found in the comprehensive process view of the Value Chain Model postulated by Michael Porter, which revolutionized the notion of the creation of services by enterprises. The ARIS Method of Prof. Scheer, together with Dr. Michael Hammer's idea of Business Process Reengineering have brought the linkages between IT and processes to the minds of companies. All three of these methods, approaches or models enable implementation of the RTE. So, even in terms of the process view, this builds upon familiar ideas - ideas, however, which now must be viewed from a holistic point of view. What is new is that the organizational considerations for an efficient enterprise must now coincide with the strategic orientation towards a focus on the customer, and with technological development as described by Gartner.

3   Processes in the RTE

The entire array of strategic advantages of the RTE can only be realized if an ERP system isolated from the external world is linked with the systems of all of the participant companies along the value-added chain. This outward-directed linkage of processes and systems necessarily entails the integration, within an enterprise, of disparate subsystems. Data management in a database, hitherto defined as an advantage of ERP systems, is difficult to accomplish in an enterprise with an RTE orientation. Subsystems such SCM or CRM, for example, are important for integration with the remaining parties involved. What falls by the wayside, then, is uniform data management in a repository, hitherto one of the main advantages of ERP systems. This inexorably leads to a paradigm shift for software manufacturers and system integrators, since the integration and automation of the various areas must take place at the process level, and not, as before, at the application level.

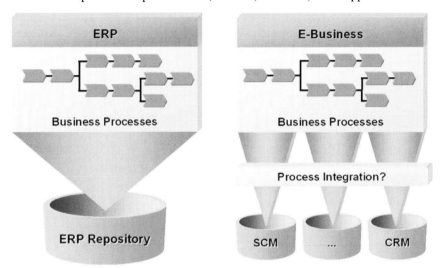

Fig. 1. The Integration Problem

One of the highest-priority tasks of the RTE, then, can be considered the savings of time and the benefits which this entails for the customer and the enterprise. This savings of time can be achieved if the enterprise operates with a uniform treatment of processes. This means both collaboration at the IT level and in standardized process design. So the mere exchange of data among levels of a company will no longer suffice. Early examples of this collaboration are the EDI systems of the 1980's and 1990's. In this regard, the Internet has made things considerably easier through open standards.

One of the key factors of success is thus collaboration at the process level. But how can such a collaborative effort be organized? The following illustration is designed to describe process management across enterprise boundaries:

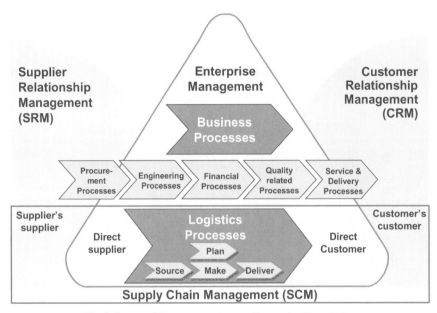

Fig. 2. Process Management Across Enterprise Boundaries

So care must be taken to ensure that processes are drawn up which can apply not just within a single enterprise but between multiple enterprises as well. That the original definitions of processes are no longer adequate here is understandable. Today, the various providers in the area of ERP software define the concept of the RTE as a pure linkage of applications within and beyond an enterprise. Many of these providers also want to offer a single, universal architecture. This is not possible as, for one, it fails to take the strategic point of view into account and, for another, it neglects the aspects of process control and improvement.

The 3-tier model by IDS Scheer AG does a very good job of linking the individual divisions of an enterprise, and of illustrating the multi-enterprise aspects of a process.

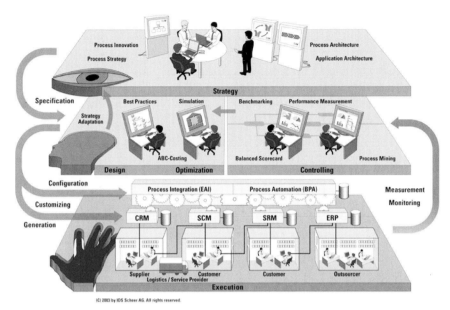

Fig. 3. Three-Tier Architecture of Business Process Excellence

This illustration also makes clear that, while in process management the application view is important for an enterprise's operational orientation, the strategic dimension, along with process design, optimization and controlling, are decisive factors in the efficient orientation of an enterprise. The ARIS Process Platform by IDS Scheer AG is of particular assistance at the second level of an enterprise. This is rounded out by the ARIS Process Performance Manager (ARIS PPM). This can be particularly helpful in terms of controlling and of ongoing improvements in processes. In the RTE concept, use of the ARIS PPM is also conceivable for performance measurement of companies participating in the RTE.

So long-term success is possible only if the disparate companies work together to replace the data repository previously in use with a process repository. This repository can then point up an optimum exploitation of potentials and lighten the load of GPA between and within companies.

4   Business Process Automation in the RTE

This gives rise to the question of how processes which are linked between companies can lead to higher benefits.

One answer to this question is Business Process Automation. There is a wealth of examples of such processes, but we would like to limit our consideration to two examples for a possible RTE/GPA architecture.

Dell, the computer manufacturer, works through a sales channel on the Internet not just to enable placement of the bulk of orders for its products; using the Internet's open standards, it is also able to facilitate communication between production facilities, process orders made to its suppliers, or participate in cross-selling.

Yet one of the main factors of Dell's success has always been the relatively low levels of inventory on hand, resulting in a pronounced decrease in capital lockup within the company.

To take an example, let us consider a customer's major order of 30,000 notebooks for a campaign with a discounter, or for a platform change at a major corporation. The concept of the RTE with GPA now contains a fully automated generation of queries to outside suppliers with capacity crosschecks, delivery deadlines and suggested pricing. Thanks to short lead times and automation, Dell can now extend its own best practice in production and order processing to cover the upstream and downstream companies as well. The result is improved communications, both with the supplier and with the shipper - and, over the long term, with the customer.

Another case study can be found in the area of the imagination. The boom unleashed by Harry Potter has not been confined to children. Along with the publishing houses, others who have profited from this boom include retailers, Internet shippers, logistics service providers, paper manufacturers and printing operations. When the fifth volume of the Harry Potter series was delivered in September 2003, 14 million copies worldwide were sent on their way to customers. This was possible, for one, due to a perfectly organized logistics operation working with superbly coordinated marketing; and, for another, as a result of processes which functioned throughout, from the manufacture of paper to the delivery to the customer. Another particular challenge, in this case, was to maintain the confidentiality of the contents, which had to be guaranteed.

Now, let us gaze into the future a little:

Harry Potter, Volume Six, is due on the shelves in two years' time. The publishing house notifies printers of the magnitude of the print run involved; these, in turn, notify paper producers of the quantity of paper which will be required, who must then either increase the production of recycled paper or commission the cutting of additional trees.

Now, if a correction needs to be made to the print run, all of the steps in this process must be repeated. With RTE and GPA, it would now be possible to have the lumberjack informed of this change automatically, since the paper producer's system automatically determines the new amounts required. Modern paper companies even place orders down to the individual tree slated for cutting.

In a subsequent step, just prior to publication, the concern then shifts to reserving appropriate levels of shipping capacity and making retailers aware of campaigns, discounts or payment deadlines. Here, automated business processes permit quick planning together with tailoring to changing framework conditions. If one imagines that the customers of Internet book dealers want to have the book in their hands the same day as customers in retail outlets, that these must then factor the order-processing lead time into the equation, it becomes clear just how elaborate an order of this nature can be. Here, where the human factor is a particularly significant source of error, RTE and GPA can offer support to prevent such mistakes.

5   Where can the RTE Concept Help an Enterprise?

The fact of the matter is that the speedy delivery of goods and services is beneficial not just to the customer of a company; since this results in improved customer relations, it is also beneficial to the company itself. The customer is increasingly prepared to pay for savings of time. Companies must approach planning, production and sales with greater flexibility, while keeping costs low at the same time. The quick delivery times of which the Internet held promise could not be realized due to the fact that old structures remained in place, or divisions were enlarged within a company with the simple appendage of an additional function. Frequently, companies already have the solutions to problems on hand but lack the time required to enact them. Emphasizing short-term, tactical decision-making, companies lose sight of long-term strategy. Without a doubt, continuous acceleration of management processes improves a company's agility. But quick decisions can only be made if there is a transparent view of the processes involved or of the key figures over which these process exert an influence. And since today it is no longer possible for a company to function as a standalone system, there is more at stake than seeing to it that all of an enterprise's divisions have access to the same up-to-date data. Today, subcontractors and suppliers must also be incorporated into the same up-to-date information flow. This is how the real-time company acts directly in the marketplace. Where delayed reactions once led to lost orders, now it lies within the grasp of the agile company to ensure itself a competitive advantage.

As indicated above, essential steps along the road to becoming an RTE include identification of processes, measurement and optimization with simultaneous automation, but also implementation of suitable IT solutions. Nevertheless, additional steps are also needed: an active approach to change management, involvement of all staff, and coordination with customers, partners and suppliers are all essential ingredients. Only a staff member who views him- or herself as a real-time worker can create the conditions prerequisite to establishing an RTE. Whoever cannot make decisions on his or her own, or cannot assume personal responsibility within a process chain, will slow down even a perfectly optimized flow. Generating an awareness of the far-reaching changes which come about when a company decides in favor of a Real-Time Enterprise approach, and offering the necessary training measures, are of the utmost importance in this regard. But the training divisions themselves must confront the new challenges they will face within the RTE framework. Whoever continues to rely on attendance-register training sessions as the sole training platform will be a loser even at the design stage. What is needed are just-in-time training approaches, and institutionalization of modern E-learning activities within the companies.

Ambitious projects can be realized only in an intelligent, step-by-step process. Soon, RTE will no longer be on a company's list of things it would be "nice to have"; it will be indispensable if the company wants to remain profitable into tomorrow.

6   Future Potentials for the RTE and the GPA

In an era demanding that IT quickly pay for itself, and in which the market is flooded with new technologies, what long-term and sustained potentials does the RTE concept have to offer? The answer is simple: all of them. The potentials must merely enter into the concept of the Real-Time Enterprise and enable genuine optimization.

In other words, cost-cutting must not be permitted to become the main goal for new technologies; instead, the main goal must be to help bring quick processes to the customer. Only the combination of these objectives can make an RTE successful.

A variety of scenarios are conceivable for the future:

- Machinery which order replacement parts and service staff through autodiagnosis
- Orders processed by mobile terminals worldwide, obviating the need for any additional worksteps, etc.
- Automated production of goods and services without requirement for instructions and/or setup times and release processes
- Product and price comparisons which can be made in the store via mobile phone

One instrument which has already been realized in relation to this technology is Fleetboard, the fleet management system for DaimlerChrysler AG, a telematic system enabling mobile loading instructions, identification of truck maintenance intervals and information exchange. Here, too, the real utility can only be realized if processes upstream and downstream are themselves real-time based, enabling the company to seize a true time advantage by reducing idle times and delivery times.

RTE means: satisfying the customer and the customer's customer. This leads to follow-up orders by loyal buyers and in the final analysis demonstrates a direct connection between King Customer and another traditional business paradigm on which RTE is based: "Time is money".

Business Process Automation is one possible response to the issue of time. Obviously, this need not inevitably have anything to do with the concept of the RTE. Still, Business Process Automation can constitute, to begin with, a first step in the right direction, and secondly, over time GPA will inevitably be connected with the success of an RTE. To generate this success, in our view, the following five steps must be taken.

Five Steps to the Real-Time Enterprise

1. Design Real-Time Processes

Existing business processes are optimized and automated from a customer and time point of view. Software tools such as the ARIS Process Platform by IDS Scheer are of assistance here.

2. Implement a Real-Time Platform

High-performance IT systems must enable direct registration, forwarding and interaction with customers and partners.

3. Adapt Software to Real-Time Processes

Application systems for ERP (Enterprise Resources Planning), CRM (Customer Relationship Management), SCM (Supply Chain Management), E-Procurement, Reporting, etc., are optimized with an eye toward providing real-time information.

4. Controlling Real-Time Processes

Current measurement of business processes, forwarding of information, comparison with specified values and benchmarks. Software tools such as the Process Performance Manager (PPM) by IDS Scheer can be used for this purpose.

5. Change Management in the Company

Ongoing transformation to become an agile, innovative and flexible enterprise, with continuous training of staff.

This is the only way to generate sustainable, long-term business success. The prerequisite for this, however, is that over the long term, the Chief Information Officer, until now more of an administrator of existing IT infrastructure, must evolve to become the Chief Process Officer, with IT not the sole guarantor of success. In this, modern BPM solutions will play an important role.

7   References

BeraterGuide – Das Jahrbuch für Beratung und Management 2004 / Andreas Gries (Hrsg.), München, H&T Verlags GmbH & Co.KG.

Die Zukunft des Managements : Perspektiven für die Unternehmensführung / Deutscher Manager-Verband e.V.. - Zürich : vdf, Hochsch.-Verl. an der ETH, 2002.

Scheer, A.-W./ Abolhassan, F./ Bosch, W.: Real-Time Enterprise – Mit beschleunigten Managementprozessen Zeit und Kosten sparen, Berlin New York u.a. 2003.

Scheer, A.-W./ Abolhassan, F./ Jost, W./ Kirchmer, M.: Business Process Excellence – ARIS in Practice, Berlin, NewYork u.a. 2002.

Scheer, A.-W./ Köppen, A.: Consulting – Wissen für die Strategie-, Prozess- und IT-Beratung, 2.Aufl., Berlin, New York u.a. 2001.

ARIS Process Platform™ and SAP NetWeaver™: Next Generation Business Process Management

Torsten Scholz
IDS Scheer AG

Karl Wagner
IDS Scheer AG

Summary

Business Process Management (BPM) projects have shown their positive impact on companies' business. Shortcomings even from successful projects and lessons learned from failed attempts lead to the conviction that BPM must now take the next deciding step.

The goal is to reduce the total cost of ownership (TCO) dramatically, to leverage existing IT investments and to raise usability and acceptance in the resulting systems.

*To develop this **Next Generation BPM**, SAP AG and IDS Scheer AG decided to combine their knowledge and their leading software in that field.*

Key Words

Business Process Management (BPM), SAP NetWeaver, Exchange Infrastructure, ARIS Process Platform, Modeling, Configuration, Execution, Controlling, ARIS for mySAP, Implementation, SAP Solution Manager

1   The Importance of Business Process Management

Nowadays, there is no longer any question that the quality of a company's business processes has a crucial impact on its sales and profits. The degree of innovation built into these business processes, as well as their flexibility and efficiency, are critically important for the success of the company. The importance of business processes is further revealed when they are considered as the link between business and IT; business applications only become business solutions when the processes are supported efficiently. The essential task of any standard business software is and always will be to provide efficient support for internal and external company processes.

To act successfully on the market, companies have to implement an efficient BPM organization with the corresponding methods, tools and underlying technologies. For any enterprise, BPM itself will become a core process.

2   What is BPM?

Successful BPM comprises 4 steps: The design, implementation, execution and controlling (measurement and evaluation) of business processes. BPM needs to be anchored in the organizational structure, requires a professional and efficient management process and demands involvement of all the relevant target groups. However, the exploitation of improvement potential thus enabled must not remain a one-off action because over the course of time only a closed loop can generate sustained and lasting competitive advantages – a genuine Business Process Lifecycle. The success of such a procedure depends on the company's process orientation and the continuity with which it is applied. This is how successful Business Process Management works.

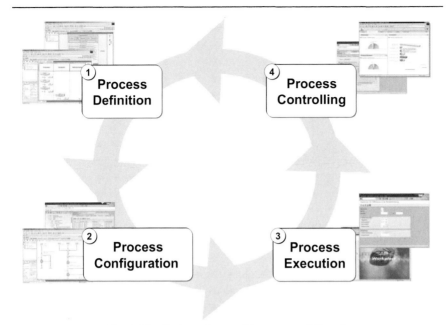

Fig. 1. The Business Process Management Lifecycle

IDS Scheer has been ranked by Gartner Group as the leading company in the field of business process management software. [cf. http://www.gartner.com/gc/weblett er/idsscheer/issue1/index.html]

ARIS means Architecture [cf. Scheer 1999]. This established and proven framework is able to cover many different approaches and methodologies such as DoDaf, Zachmann, IDEF and others.

There is a huge variety of different projects that were successfully realized with ARIS. For example:

- E- Business/E-Commerce
- Supply Chain Management (SCM)/Customer Relationship Management (CRM)
- Business Process Reengineering (BPR)
- Balanced Score Card (BSC)
- Cost cutting/Cost analyzing
- Risk Management
- Sarbanes Oxeley Act
- Activity-Based Costing

- Quality Management
- Knowledge Management
- (ERP) Software Implementation
- Enterprise Application Integration (EAI) w/o Web Services
- (Object-oriented) Software Engineering

Some projects are described for example in the book *Business Process Excellence - ARIS in Practice* [cf. Scheer et al. 2002]. This shows all the different colors of process management, some with a technical background and others without.

3   Where is BPM Today?

The BPM initiatives of the last years have shown their positive impact on companies' business. At least a reduction in complexity and cost cutting-effects were noticeable. The more BPM itself was handled as a process and was implemented into companies' organization, the more benefit could be derived from those projects. But for midsize companies in particular, this upfront investment might pose a hurdle to addressing this subject.

On the other hand, there have also been many projects in this field that failed or did not reveal the expected benefits.

What were the risk factors?

- Technology-driven approach
- Missing and error-prone communication between stakeholders and project members, especially business and IT people
- Late involvement of operational departments
- A lack of management commitment
- Choosing the wrong technology

to mention only a few.

These risks could lead to

- Numerous iterations

- Systems that do not support business processes

- No end-user acceptance

- A lack of flexibility in the resulting IT system

- High maintenance costs to support further process changes

- Cost, time and budget overruns

Even if the project was successfully completed, there would always be a feeling that you could exploit IT systems more effectively.

Many of these problems could be attributed to

- The lack of a unified business language (methodology) and procedural model for all project members

- Tools, methods and technologies in each phase coming from different providers and not fitting together

There is obviously a lot of potential for reducing the TCO of BPM, leveraging IT investments and improving usability and end-user acceptance. Solving these problems will improve existing BPM solutions and open this must-have for midsize companies as well.

4   Next Generation BPM

Up until now, process modeling and standard software have represented two different worlds.

SAP AG, the world's leading provider of business software solutions, and IDS Scheer AG, the leading provider of tools and methods for process management, decided to create a comprehensive solution for business process management. IDS Scheer's ARIS Process Platform will be integrated into SAP NetWeaver™, the open integration and application platform, to provide customers with a comprehensive BPM solution – and thus with a completely integrated process platform. For the first time, customers will have the ability to connect the modeling and optimization of business processes with the physical configuration and execution of these processes.

With the integration of ARIS Process Platform in SAP NetWeaver, these two worlds are combined in such a way that in future, business processes rather than the software technology will be the focus of attention.

An enterprise can rely on a proven and unified business language – a methodology – and a procedural model covering the whole lifecycle of a business process. The leading SAP technology and business applications give the advantage they seek.

In the past, the business process logic was tightly interwoven with the application logic, but this has changed dramatically. With the SAP NetWeaver integration and application platform, SAP has developed a new foundation for the mySAP Business Suite. One of the most important innovations in this technology platform is the separation of the application functionality from the business process logic. At the same time, the logic of the business processes is no longer encoded in SAP NetWeaver; instead it is configured using new standards such as BPML (Business Process Modeling Language) [cf. http://www.bpmi.org/specifications.esp] or BPEL (Business Process Execution Language) [cf. http://www.webservices.org/]. This new technology represents enormous progress in the software's agility and its ability to respond quickly and efficiently to users' process requirements. This means that in future, companies will be able to adapt software to new process requirements much more easily and cheaply. Beyond that, the solution also enables the technical integration of third-party and legacy systems.

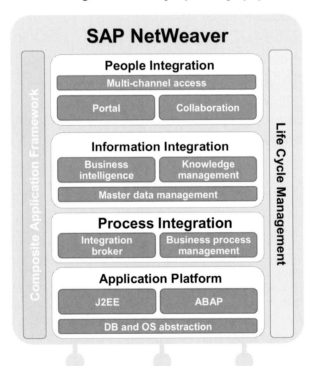

Fig. 2. SAP NetWeaver™ Platform

The entire business process management lifecycle is undergirded by the combined strengths of SAP and IDS Scheer. A direct connection is established between business and technical models on the one hand and the software executing them on the other. The closed loop, which extends from the business process analysis and the business process model through process configuration and execution to controlling, enables continuous improvement of all the business processes in use in a company. In practical terms, this means faster operational rollout, continuous improvement of business processes in operation, and consequently the best possible use of the SAP system's enormous application capabilities.

5   What is the Vision?

The solution integrated in SAP NetWeaver provides a modeling environment based on the ARIS Process Platform, with a standardized storage area – the process repository – which includes all business-related and technological (execution level) model information. Here, the modeling environment provides various views in support of SAP NetWeaver Exchange Infrastructure processes, Unified Modeling Language (UML) diagrams, process chains, or SAP Solution Maps, for example.

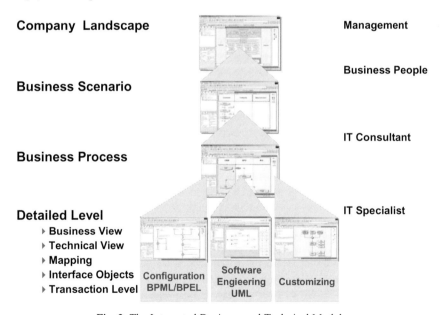

Fig. 3. The Integrated Business and Technical Models

The solution integrated in SAP NetWeaver includes four components: The first enables free, visual modeling of business processes, whereas with the second, application processes can be configured. The third component is used to illustrate responsibility for execution, including monitoring and alarm functions, and an event management facility. The fourth component, which deals with process controlling, focuses on statistical indices and their analysis. In this way, the user can monitor both the efficiency and the effectiveness of the business processes being executed, i.e. workflows as well as cross-component and cross-company processes.

The benefits of a unified modeling environment for businesspersons and IT specialists with seamless integration into the execution engine are obvious. This dramatically reduces the effort in terms of time and cost, not only during the initial process configuration when the system is implemented but also for operation and continuous monitoring and improvement. The models of the transaction processes can be changed quickly, with the methods required for software implementation delivered at the same time. This shortens response time and raises the quality of the business processes supported by the software.

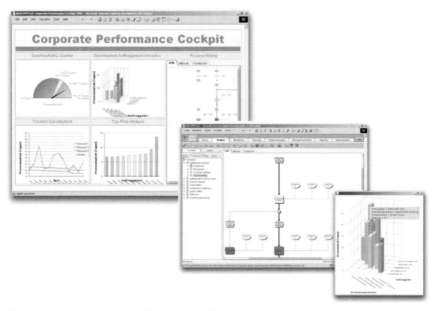

Fig. 4. Process Performance Measurement With ARIS Also Addresses Cross-Component and Cross-Enterprise Processes

The result is shorter cycles in response to process changes, from the concept to configuration and controlling, the associated cost savings, and a greater pool of knowledge within the company.

Whether users are concerned with modeling, configuration, execution or controlling – it is always one and the same process, and it is managed in one and the same repository. Consequently, there is no storage of redundant data.

6   The Future Starts Today

The constituent parts of the new solution are already available today. This allows BPM projects to be started right now. Existing ARIS business models can later be transferred to the new SAP NetWeaver platform without difficulty. The link to the technical models can be prepared as well. This means that companies can begin reaping all the advantages of a consistent business process management system today with ARIS, ARIS for mySAP, ARIS UML Designer and ARIS Process Performance Manager, and transfer all their process information to SAP Net-Weaver at a later date.

7   References

http://www.bpmi.org/specifications.esp

http://www.gartner.com/gc/webletter/idsscheer/issue1/index.html

http://www.webservices.org/

Scheer, A.-W., Abolhassan, F., Jost, W., Kirchmer, M. (ed.): Business Process Excellence – ARIS in Practice. Berlin, New York, and others 2002.

Scheer, A.-W.: ARIS – Business Process Frameworks. 3rd edition, Berlin, New York and others 1999.

Dynamic and Mobile Business Process Management

Donald Steiner
WebV2, Inc.

Summary

This chapter provides an overview of the application of a combined business process modeling, business process execution, and business rule execution framework to solve a delivery planning problem in the supply-chain management area. Human decision-makers, automated decision-making systems and software systems are coordinated in a business process to effectively deal with and respond to late changes to orders by customers.

Key Words

Business Process Management, Supply Chain, Intelligent Agents, Business Rules, Web Services, Mobile Solutions

1   Project Background

ARIS is used as a tool for modeling business processes. Processes are modeled in ARIS by a graphical user interface that allows a user to define the individual tasks of a process and specify their interdependencies. Processes defined in ARIS can be exported into the Business Process Management (BPML) standard for representing business processes. This BPML representation can then be executed by a variety of process execution engines.

In particular, WebV2, Inc., provides a process execution engine that enables the federation of distributed systems and applications as well as the mobility of the workforce. WebV2's *ProcessCoupler™* approach is to provide each participating node (software system or human user) with a lightweight software wrapper. Each ProcessCoupler wrapper is capable of executing a business process in its own right and is, in particular, responsible for that part (role) of the process with which the node is associated. This allows processes to be executed across a distributed system without the requirement of the traditional central server. ProcessCoupler wrappers automatically synchronize the process execution while still providing for centralized control and monitoring of the entire system.

Gensym Corp. provides the *G2* business rules engine that automates complex decision-making. G2 enables the representation, simulation, and execution of business rules to cope with the changing demands of a complex business environment.

Using ARIS, G2, and the WebV2 ProcessCoupler solution together, businesses have a complete solution for modeling and executing business processes and business rules in a combined environment. Figure 1 depicts how these products interrelate.

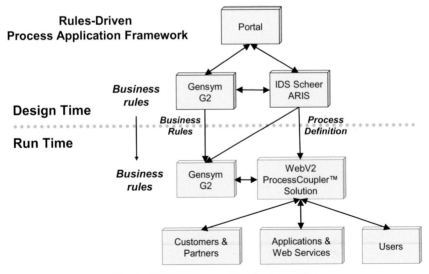

Fig. 1. G2/ARIS/ProcessCoupler Interaction

This chapter describes the use of a combined ARIS/G2/ProcessCoupler solution to solve a problem occurring within supply-chain management in the high-tech manufacturing area. In the current dynamic business environment, it is common for customers to change their orders late in the supply-chain lifecycle – sometimes shortly before shipment or even during shipment of the order! In this case, the handling of the orders managed by an enterprise resource planning (ERP) system must be re-evaluated to ensure optimal inventory throughput. This involves a number of systems within the enterprise, including the ERP system and various human decision makers, as well as corresponding systems at the customer end. Some of the users may be mobile using occasionally connected computing.

In this case study, we show how the distributed business process solution offered by WebV2 was used in conjunction with the G2 rules engine and the ARIS modeling environment, to reduce days of inventory caused by late order changes.

The results of this project were presented at the Supply Chain World 2003 conference (cf. Brown 2003) and are also described by Paul Harmon of Business Process Trends (cf. Harmon 2003).

2   Project Goals

The primary goal of the project was to show a demonstrable reduction in days-of-inventory when faced with a highly dynamic demand and frequent order changes, while ensuring delivery performance according to increasingly stringent service-level agreements.

From a technical point of view, the aim of the project was to demonstrate the ability to rapidly model, validate, implement and continuously improve business processes involving human users and machine systems across distributed environments – indeed, even separated by firewalls and occasionally connected networks.

The overall architecture for the developed system is depicted in figure 2.

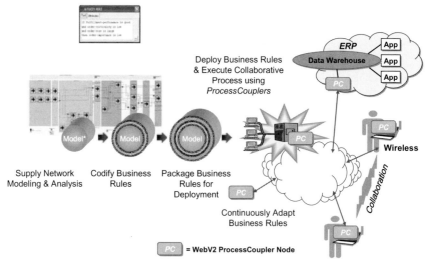

Fig. 2. Delivery Planning Architecture

3   Procedure

To date, work in supply-chain modeling, validation with simulation, and online deployment of supply-chain planning systems has shown that these tools help to realize substantial improvements in supply-chain performance once they are deployed. Effective design techniques ensure that system dynamics are accommodated while supply-chain flexibility and responsiveness are increased. However, putting new designs into practice remains difficult. Continuous improvement still involves substantial offline analysis and system reformulation to adapt to changing circumstances.Companies need better technology to drive improvements in existing supply-chain planning systems in an environment of rapid change. The ARIS / G2 / PC solution addresses this need directly by adding robustness to the design methodology and speed to the task of migrating a selected design into operation.

Figure 3 highlights the methodology adopted by the project team. *Design* comprises activities of elucidating the business rules from experts, defining business processes and identifying resources (people or machines) that are affected by the proposed changes. ARIS Design Platform and methodologies play an important role in helping developers, information providers and users to rapidly model the processes and identify the rules that need to be automated. *Validation* is a key risk-reduction step but is only useful if developers complete this step quickly and with minimal data. Dynamic simulation technology is incorporated into the methodology along with systematic procedures to reduce reliance on data that may not exist and eliminate the tendency to over-analyze. The result is a greatly reduced risk of implementation, higher acceptance, and greater transfer of information to managers, decision-makers and other stakeholders in the success of the transformation. *Deployment* is the important step of migrating the business rules and processes into operation. The tool suite is built upon virtual machine software environments that allows for on-the-fly modification, which means that moving the design into an execution environment does not require an application re-write. Business rules developed in the design environment are identical to those used in development and for validation.

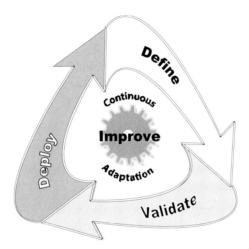

Fig. 3. Design/Validation/Deployment Lifecycle

The project was conducted in two major phases incorporating modeling and implementing the required business rules and business processes.

3.1 Modeling, Validation, and Implementation of Business Rules

First and foremost was the analysis and modeling of the business rules required for dealing with late order changes. The project team selected the Supply Chain Operations Reference (SCOR) model and methodology of the Supply Chain Council to facilitate designing the business rules. The SCOR model describes supply-chain processes at a high level and has the important advantage of linking processes to best practices and key performance indicators that guide users towards achieving the goals of supply-chain transformation projects. The SCOR model has been adopted as a standard within many companies and is used widely for understanding existing processes and creating new ones. SCOR lowers the risk of implementing a transformation and accelerates the rate of change to new processes.

The high-tech manufacturer specified that the business rules must mimic the expertise used by expert planners, as this was known to result in an effective re-allocation of orders among supply points. In addition, the automated system was required to make the business rules explicit so that they could be examined and understood by developers and decision-makers. Finally, it was specified that explanation must be available so that it was clear why a specific re-allocation of an order was made, just as would be required of human planners. Members of the project team interviewed planners at the high-tech manufacturer to capture their domain knowledge. Partial results of these interviews are shown in figure 4, which shows the decision space for determining the capability of a specific shipping point to deliver a certain customer's order based on *responsiveness* and current *inventory availability*, both of which are metrics maintained in real time. As shown in figure 4, when the responsiveness to the customer is good and there is plenty of inventory on hand, the 'capability' of that shipping point to deliver the order is considered 'good'. Decision spaces such as these were developed with input from planners as a basis and mapped directly into natural language rules that were entered into the business rules framework and validated within the context of the specific high-tech manufacturing supply network.

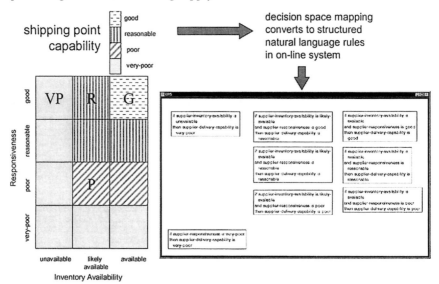

Fig. 4. Decision Space for Order Reallocation

3.2 Modeling and Implementation of Business Processes

Secondly, the business process was established linking the various players (people and software) in the system.

The following describes the process at a high level by listing the primary tasks that are performed and their sequencing. Note that this description is independent of the components that perform the tasks. These details can be determined a priori or, with an optimal dynamic execution environment, automatically at run time, based on the services the components offer. The steps are:

1. Initiating the process by request or according to a specified schedule.

2. Retrieving the current set of orders from the ERP system. The sets of orders selected are those for which the ERP system has already published a delivery note, which identified an optimal supply point, but have not yet left the supply point. The ERP delivery note is published close to the shipment date, which means that orders examined by this system typically fall within a day or two of their shipment date.

3. Modifying the shipment point of each order in the set based on the business rules and human user input of order criticality.

4. Updating the change order set into the ERP system.

In particular, the generation of the modified change order set requires collaboration among the business rules engine, a number of human users and enterprise systems (located both within the enterprise and at the customer). This leads to the problem of how to coordinate this decision-making process.

ARIS was used for modeling the processes. As the goal of the project was to generate processes that could be directly executable, it was decided to use BPML as a representation format. Accordingly, the eEPC and eEPC(Column) means of process representation in ARIS were chosen for modeling, as they can be directly output into BPML (cf. Arkin 2002). The eEPC mechanism enables sequences of functions and events to be defined. Functions represent a BPML service. Functions can also define input and output data. Events represent the current state. Functions and events are linked together by a number of ARIS constructs such as AND, OR, and XOR. These can in turn be used to define conditionals and loops. The eEPC(Column) mechanism of ARIS enables roles of a business process to be defined. The roles are automatically output in BPML 'locate' constructs. Subprocesses can be very easily defined within ARIS by creating a link from a function to another process. It was very easy to represent the processes within ARIS. However, it must be noted that not all ARIS models can generate executable BPML processes. The designer of the process must take into consideration the resulting implementation. For example, conditional data is represented as the name of an event.

Figure 5 depicts a simplified model of the Change Order process as represented in ARIS. Figure 6 shows the equivalent representation of the process in BPML that was automatically generated by ARIS.

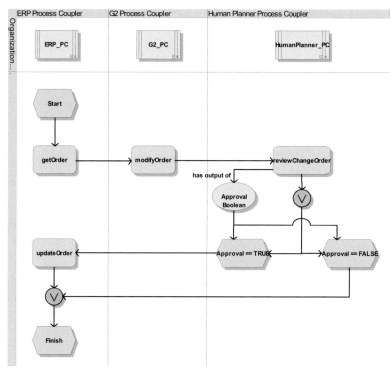

Fig. 5. : ARIS Model of Change Order Process

```
<bpml:process name="ChangeOrder">

    <bpml:context>
        <bpml:property name="Approval" type="xsd:boolean"/>
    </bpml:context>

    <bpml:sequence>
        <bpml:action name="getOrder" locate="ERP_PC"/>
        <bpml:action name="modifyOrder" locate="G2_PC"/>
        <bpml:action name="reviewChangeOrder" locate="HumanPlanner_PC">
            <bpml:output parameter="xsd:boolean">
                <bpml:source property="Approval"/>
            </bpml:output>
        </bpml:action>
        <bpml:all>
            <bpml:switch>
                <bpml:case>
                    <bpml:condition>
                        Approval == TRUE
                    </bpml:condition>
                    <bpml:sequence>
                        <bpml:action name="updateOrder" locate="ERP_PC"/>
                    </bpml:sequence>
                </bpml:case>
            </bpml:switch>
            <bpml:switch>
                <bpml:case>
                    <bpml:condition>
                        Approval == FALSE
                    </bpml:condition>
                    <bpml:sequence>
                    </bpml:sequence>
                </bpml:case>
            </bpml:switch>
        </bpml:all>
    </bpml:sequence>
</bpml:process>
```

Fig. 6. BPML Representation of Change Order Process

The WebV2 ProcessCoupler™ architecture enabled the resulting BPML representation of the process to be developed and deployed rapidly and effectively. The following provides an overview of the architecture and functionality of the WebV2 solution.

4   Enabling Loose Coupling

WebV2 provides the leading decentralized business process execution and collaboration framework with their ProcessCoupler™ solution. The ProcessCoupler architecture provides a loosely coupled connectivity solution across applications and human users. This enables low-cost development/deployment, rapid change management, as well as support for mobility.

The decentralized nature of the ProcessCoupler deployment allows for executing business processes where centralized business process execution engines may be impractical or impossible. This occurs, for example, where trading partners (customers and/or suppliers) want seamless integration of business processes into their own back-end systems.

The WebV2 ProcessCoupler software provides and supports the latest Web Services standards (e.g. SOAP, UDDI, WSDL, BPEL). They also support the execution of business processes described by BPEL4WS. They can also interact with Web Services as back-end applications, thereby enhancing web services with the ability to dynamically join and participate in existing and future business processes. However, currently, Business Process Management across Web Services is still very tightly coupled – the supplied interfaces are highly dependent upon the chosen architecture and business processes. The ProcessCoupler software enables Web Service interfaces to be independent of the actual business processes, architecture, and implementation details. This enables Web Services to be integrated into business processes much more quickly, dynamically, and cost-effectively.

Occasionally Connected Computing (OCC) has been described as a key enabler for the real-time enterprise. As the mobility of workers and computing environments becomes increasingly important to the enterprise, work is often done offline and must be seamlessly integrated with the enterprise when a connection is re-established. This requires the ability to support asynchronous connectivity to business processes.

WebV2's ProcessCoupler solution enables asynchronous participation of applications and human users in business processes. As the solution is lightweight and based on pure Java, it runs on mobile devices (e.g. PocketPC). This enables easy mobilization of the enterprise and incorporation of mobile devices in the enterprise and its business processes. The ProcessCoupler node is aware of the process and its state and context – even while disconnected.

WebV2's Business Process Execution solution allows abstracting the domain-specific details of a business process from the domain-independent mechanisms used to carry out the process. This provides a number of advantages:

- The business-process owner can concentrate solely on defining the business process and not worry about underlying technical architectural details.

- Underlying process components providing enterprise functionality can be provided as highly reusable patterns.

- New sub-processes can be added dynamically and independently of the original process. This enables additional processes to be easily defined for selecting and negotiating among additional applications.

- Underlying services can be dynamically added, replaced, and/or changed within a running system and be immediately accessible – without changing the business process or changing any part of the existing runtime system. This greatly simplifies and largely automates change management, both during initial system development and deployment and during ongoing change.

Furthermore, the resulting system is independent of the following IT choice points:

- Underlying message transport infrastructure (e.g. asynchronous or synchronous; point-to-point or broadcast; TCP/IP, HTTP, JMS or other third-party offerings)

- Security and authentication procedures (e.g. use of Public Key Infrastructure)

- Transaction and logging procedures

- Architecture – where subsystems are actually deployed

This means that any desired IT approach can be integrated (at any time) without changing the original business process.

Each node in the system is represented by ProcessCoupler software that is capable of executing a process in accordance with a common process definition (e.g. BPEL4WS). ProcessCoupler nodes are able to dynamically discover each other across enterprise networks and synchronize the execution of the process steps with each other. The ProcessCoupler software interacts with back-end applications via standards (e.g. JCA, JDBC or Web Services) as well as via third-party data adapters. The ProcessCoupler software interacts with human users via web interface, standalone interfaces, or existing application (e.g. Microsoft Excel). Figure 7 shows an overview of the ProcessCoupler Service Oriented Architecture.

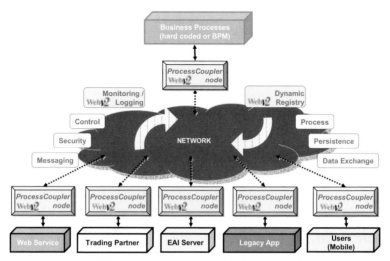

Fig. 7. ProcessCoupler Service Oriented Architecture

Furthermore, ProcessCoupler nodes are actually able to directly execute a business process without using a centralized BPMS! (cf. figure 8) This grid-based alternative, or peer-to-peer approach, reduces reliance on expensive, heavyweight servers and communication bottlenecks. It configures automatically and is adaptable to any IT infrastructure.

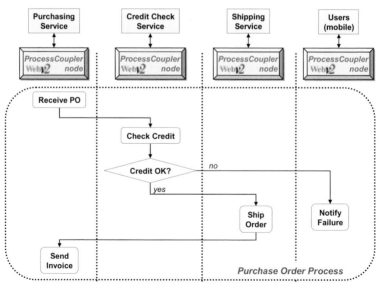

Fig. 8. Decentralized Process Execution

4.1 Interaction Processes

A powerful feature of WebV2's process execution solution is the ability to support highly reusable application-independent sub-processes, or so-called interaction processes, that can be used in conjunction with the original business process.

For example, suppose the original business process is designed for accessing a single service provider for a given task. The business may decide that it can gain significant advantage by selecting dynamically from a range of possible service providers, based on certain criteria, such as best price, quality of service, availability, etc. Without changing the original business process, the ProcessCoupler node can select dynamically (at run time) which service to invoke. This is handled by a specialized *contracting* interaction pattern.

The interaction processes are built upon the semantically rich communication and coordination standards developed by the Foundation for Intelligent Physical Agents (FIPA). In particular, FIPA defines higher level message types (cf. FIPA 2002) that go beyond the usual request/response interaction. These message types include agree (to perform the task), refuse (to perform the task), query (for information), inform (information), cfp (call-for proposals), bid, accept (a bid), and reject (a bid). FIPA also specifies a means for representing possible sequences of such message types into Interaction Protocols (IPs), and a library of common IPs, such as FIPA-request (similar to client-server) or FIPA-contract-net.

Interaction processes enable

- interaction concerning the task to be performed before it is actually invoked,

- sharing the context of the process, and

- incorporation of transaction, security, and monitoring processes without changing underlying interfaces, arguments, or processes.

The rich set of communication forms, and interaction processes allow business analysts to specify which services they want easily and rapidly as well as the way they want them delivered.

Furthermore, interaction processes can be dynamically nested, allowing seamless incorporation of new processes and contexts supporting enterprise functionality, such as those managing security, authentication, or transactions. This is accomplished without changing the underlying application services or their interfaces.

Interaction processes cover the following functionalities:

- Enterprise functionality (e.g. security, two-phase commit)

- IT functionality (e.g. monitoring, control)

- Process execution strategies (e.g. round-robin, multi-server)

- Negotiation mechanisms (e.g. sealed-bid contracting, auction)

- Service discovery mechanisms (e.g. brokered, brokerless)

- Underlying exception-handling guidance

4.2 Mobilization of Business Processes

Occasionally Connected Computing (OCC) has been described as a key enabler for the real-time enterprise. As mobility of workers and computing environments becomes increasingly important to the enterprise, work is often done offline, and must be seamlessly integrated with the enterprise when a connection is re-established. This requires the ability to support asynchronous connectivity to business processes.

WebV2's solution enables the asynchronous participation of applications and human users in business processes. As the solution is lightweight and based on pure Java, it runs on heterogeneous platforms, including mobile devices (e.g. PocketPC). This enables easy mobilization of the enterprise and incorporation of mobile devices in the enterprise and its business processes.

A major component of business process automation and workflow solutions is the integration of the human user. Of increasing importance is the ability to support the human user in an asynchronous fashion, as required by mobile and occasionally connected environments. WebV2's ProcessCoupler software can be installed directly on a user's mobile device. This solution provides the following features:

1. Users of mobile devices can be integrated with enterprise business processes in a manner that is significantly less difficult than standard portal-based solutions. All device-specific and user-specific files and information are stored and maintained only by the device. This allows for seamless scalability to thousands of users without any extra hardware resources. A burden with portal-based solutions is that the portal must maintain all communication and interface possibilities for each device and user (e.g. WAP, screen resolutions, ...). This, in turn, inhibits scalability and maintenance.

2. The ProcessCoupler node is aware of the process and its state and context – even while disconnected. The user can interact with the ProcessCoupler software (and thereby in the context of the process) while offline. Upon reconnection, the ProcessCoupler node automatically continues the process. This applies even if the IP address of the device changes. Any change in the IP address of the device is automatically re-registered with the ProcessCoupler network. The ProcessCoupler software also has direct access to any data stored on the user's device. Any delivered information, and the display of the information, can be tailored to the user's context.

3. Direct device-to-device (peer-to-peer) data and process interaction among users across mobile devices as well as interaction with applications on the fixed net.

4. Multi-modal user interaction via one or more of the following:

- Existing standard application (e.g. Microsoft Excel): The ProcessCoupler software uses back-end connectivity to the application – transmitting the data to the application – which uses its built-in interfaces for presentation to and interaction with the user.

- Standard HTML browser: The ProcessCoupler solution provides a local web server. Changing the user interface is as simple as replacing a few html files and can be done while the ProcessCoupler node is running.

- Customized Java application: A dedicated graphical user interface can be built and deployed as a separately running application.

5. Interaction across the ProcessCoupler network and with net-based applications via Web Services standards. The ProcessCoupler software supports UDDI registry, SOAP interaction, and participation in BPEL4WS-based processes.

6. Automatic update of run-time software upon change (from external repository). This can occur either by regular polling or pushing. This significantly reduces maintenance overhead.

7. Ability to interact with software while offline; when back online, software resumes interaction with fixed net.

WebV2 currently supports ProcessCoupler software running on any device which runs the J2ME Personal Profile (cf. Courtney 2002).

4.3 Web Services

The WebV2 solution embraces and extends current and planned Web Service standards. In particular, the solution leverages standards-based business process languages, such as BPEL4WS (Business Process Execution Language for Web Services), under standardization by OASIS (cf. Andrews et. al. 2003).
Web Services are supported by the WebV2 solution in the following ways:

- A ProcessCoupler node can invoke an external web service to accomplish a task in the process.

- This allows a web service to be encapsulated by ProcessCoupler software as a back-end application in its own right.

- ProcessCoupler nodes enable their back-end applications to be offered as web services to the outside world.

- Business processes executed by ProcessCoupler nodes can be offered as web services.

BPEL provides mechanisms for representing a business process and for defining the interfaces which a web service must provide in order to participate in the business process. The ProcessCoupler software is able to execute a process represented by BPEL.

4.4 Infrastructure

The ProcessCoupler solution also offers domain-independent services required to facilitate the execution of business processes.

This includes:

• Registration of services

• Finding ProcessCoupler nodes which perform services

• Enterprise functionality, such as security, authentication, persistence

Specialized ProcessCoupler nodes supporting this functionality include:

Directory Facilitator: This service maintains a registry of services offered by other ProcessCoupler nodes. The functionality is similar to a "real-time runtime UDDI"

Monitor: This service provides a centralized history of all communication (i.e. messages sent from and received by) corresponding to a given ProcessCoupler node or set of ProcessCoupler nodes. This functionality is obtained by running a monitor interaction protocol that requires all participants to copy the received and sent messages to the monitor.

5   Results

The business process management solution demonstrated a 66% reduction in inventory costs while meeting or exceeding customer service level agreement expectations. This has profound impact in a multi-million dollar business! These results are currently under review by the customer and it is expected that the results will be phased into the manufacturing environment.

Furthermore, the rapid development and implementation showed that the combined ARIS/G2/WebV2 modeling and execution approach can reduce the cost of deployment by up to 50% and the cost of change by up to 80%. This was modeled according to an industry supply-chain reference model, simulated, verified and deployed in order to manage more efficiently the repercussions in late order changes from customers to reduce inventory and meet ever-more stringent customer service level agreements. Business processes linking ERP, business rules engine, and human decision makers using OCC mobile devices were deployed on an automated basis.

6   References

Andrews, T., Curbera, F., Dholakia, H.,Goland, Y., Klein, J., Leymann, F., Liu, K., Roller, D., Smith, D., Thatte, S. (Ed.), Trickovic, I., Weerawarana, S.: Business Process Execution Language for Web Services Version 1.1. BEA Systems, International Business Machines Corporation, Microsoft Corporation, SAP AG, Siebel Systems. 2003.

Arkin, A.: Business Process Modeling Language. BPMI.org. 2002

Brown, G.: Deploying Delivery Planning Business Rules Through Web Services. Supply Chain World North America. Atlanta. April 2003.

Courtney, J.: Personal Profile Specification. JSR 62. Java Community Process. 2002.

FIPA: Communicative Act Library Specification. The Foundation for Intelligent Physical Agents. 2002.

Harmon, P.: Intel's Real-Time Delivery Planning Application. A BP Trends Case Study. April 2003.

IDS Scheer AG (Ed.): ARIS BPML Interface. IDS Scheer Technical White Paper. September 2003.

Supply Chain Council (Ed.): Supply-Chain Operations Reference-model (SCOR), Version 4.0. 2002

WebV2., Inc. (Ed.): Dynamic and Mobile Federated Business Process Execution. WebV2 Whitepaper. November, 2003.

Automation of Manufacturing Support Processes at a Mid-Market Manufacturing Company, Utilizing SAP Solutions

Ed Brady
American Meter, Inc.

Marc Scharsig
IDS Scheer, Inc.

Summary

Traditional manufacturing process automation initiatives have focused on direct manufacturing value-added activities (assembly, fabrication, material handling, etc). Logically, these activities are easiest to measure, to describe, to pinpoint deficiencies and to calculate improvement/ROI from automation projects. With the maturing of ERP software solutions and associated implementation methodologies, process automation projects can be successfully applied to white-collar support processes (accounting, customer service, production planning and control, supply chain management) as well. This case study illustrates the efforts to automate manufacturing support processes, using the SAP software solution, at the American Meter group of companies.

Key Words

ERP Implementation, Process-oriented ERP, White-collar Business Process Automation, SAP Standard Software, ARIS Process Modeling

1   Project Background

1.1 Introduction

American Meter Company is in the second year of a five-year plan to overhaul its IT capabilities. The project described in this article involves a preliminary phase of implementing a new ERP system. The project scope was to implement a set of "to-be" processes, which were defined in an earlier, enterprise-wide business process-reengineering project, using SAP standard ERP software, at a "1st article" division, which represents a cross-section of the processes within the group.

1.2 Company Background

American Meter (AMCO) has been a leader in the measurement and control of natural gas since the very beginning of the industry. Today, AMCO continues to fulfill that role as a member of ELSTER-AMCO. This global organization brings the latest technology and best practices from leading European and American manufacturers of gas measurement and control equipment to markets around the world.

AMCO has a history of designing innovations that have consistently improved the accuracy and service life of gas meters, and has established the industry standards for long-term accuracy and reliability.

This organization has several world-class manufacturing facilities around North America for its broad-based product lines.

Looking to the future, AMCO continues to invest in the development of innovative products and services for the natural gas industry. These investments will ensure that they are able to continue to provide their customers with the very best value in gas measurement and control.

American Meter Company consists of 6 legal entities in 3 countries, primarily servicing the Americas region. We have 13 plant locations, which manufacture and offer a portfolio of products and services to the gas distribution market. A product model of current company offerings is shown in figure 1. The company uses a direct sales model to reinforce its long-standing relationship with the utility industry. The company employs approximately 1400, and anticipates ~350 ERP users.

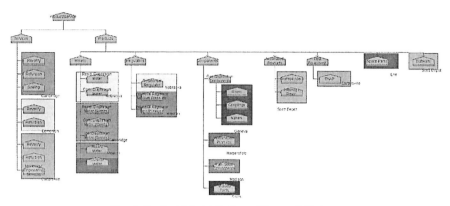

Fig. 1. Product Model Reflects Diverse Offerings

Organizationally, the company is structured around semi-autonomous divisions which manufacture exclusive product lines. Business models and manufacturing strategy employed by the plants range from configure-to-order to make-to-stock and repetitive manufacturing in mixed mode, as illustrated in the enterprise process model (figure 2).

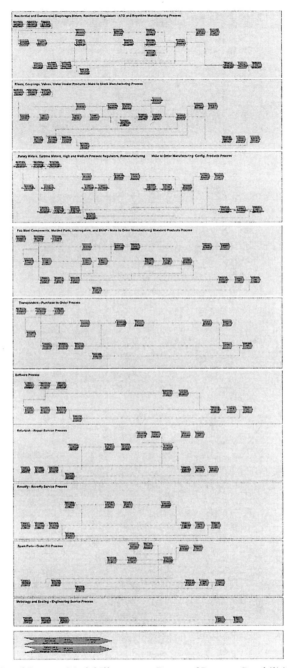

Fig. 2. Top-Level Process Model Illustrates a Range of Process Capabilities to Support Diverse Product and Service Offerings

1.3 Business Conditions

Market dynamics in the utility industry have driven virtually all major players to refocus on cost efficiency. While this represents a risk, for American Meter companies it also provides an opportunity to streamline administrative business processes and to introduce additional services to provide value and increase customer satisfaction. A considerable amount of manufacturing optimization has already been accomplished to satisfy these objectives. The fact that most of the core business information resides in several different Enterprise Resource Planning (ERP) systems, which are inherently closed and impede common process leverage, makes replacing them with a single integrated ERP system the next high-leverage enabler of continuous improvement.

1.4 Project Motivation

As we completed the process analysis and reengineering phase of our ERP initiative, we started to realize, at all levels of the organization, how much improvement opportunity existed throughout the enterprise if we could propagate a continuous drive toward operational excellence in our administrative processes. The ERP software selection and RFP project gave us reason to be optimistic that current-generation standard software such as SAP could provide the first major boost in this direction. The implementation of a live system, using our defined "to-be" processes, would initialize the adoption of external best practices, inter-company collaboration, and a culture of continuous process improvement, in addition to the first-generation "fixes" enabled by the first fresh look at process change in a decade.

1.5 Project History

Several projects have been undertaken to study the strategic information technology options and feasibility of an enterprise-wide deployment of an integrated ERP system to consolidate core business information and to leverage common business processes. The ERP initiative was selected on the basis of total cost, risk, and flexibility with respect to strategic business plans. Projects to define enterprise-wide "to-be" processes, select ERP software and construct a pilot prototype of the ERP solution have been successfully completed. The executive board approved an ERP system implementation project, which will demonstrate the improvements associated with a "backbone" of common processes, underlying discrete distributed operating units.

1.6 Summary of the Automation Solution

As depicted in figure 3, the projected solution incorporates a higher degree of process automation in the following functions: Order Entry, Production Planning and Control, Material Management, Accounting. Other administrative and manufacturing support process areas (Quality Management, Plant Maintenance, Human Resources) were determined to have lower immediate benefit for the enterprise, and automation of these processes was postponed to a subsequent project.

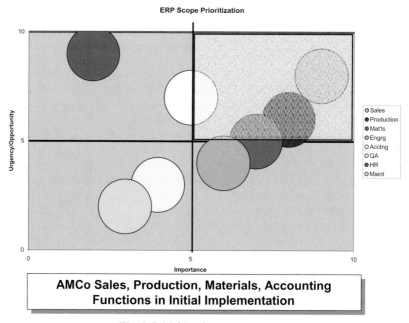

Fig. 3. Initial Implementation Scope

1.7 Summary of the Entire Process/IT Architecture

The IT strategy is to automate tasks with high transaction intensity and process repeatability, so that the professionals involved can devote more of their available time and energy to in-depth analysis and proactive performance. This strategy applies equally to IT tasks and customer service, production planning and control, accounting and other administrative processes. It requires deployment of current, standard IT tools enabling simplified, streamlined, integrated and reliable information flow, but tools which at the same time are mature enough to ensure 1st-time successful implementation.

2   Project Goals

The objectives of the AMCO ERP project revolve around enabling and realizing the case for change (figure 4). The ERP project is providing a forcing function, or catalyst, for process and structural improvements across the enterprise, which will position the American Meter companies to effectively compete in the 21st century.

Case for Change...

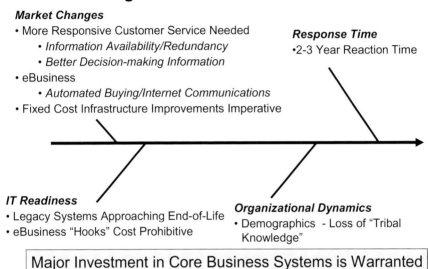

Market Changes
- More Responsive Customer Service Needed
  - *Information Availability/Redundancy*
  - *Better Decision-making Information*
- eBusiness
  - *Automated Buying/Internet Communications*
- Fixed Cost Infrastructure Improvements Imperative

Response Time
- 2-3 Year Reaction Time

IT Readiness
- Legacy Systems Approaching End-of-Life
- eBusiness "Hooks" Cost Prohibitive

Organizational Dynamics
- Demographics - Loss of "Tribal Knowledge"

Major Investment in Core Business Systems is Warranted

Fig. 4. Case for Change

2.1 Corporate Objectives

- To sustain market leadership in residential gas meters.

- To continue producing top-of-the-line quality products.

- To enhance profitability.

- To improve operational excellence, increasing organizational effectiveness and process efficiency.

- To increase business activities in the more profitable/growth market segments.

- To reposition AMCO as a prime utility industry supplier, recognized for being easy to do business with and for being responsive to the changing needs of the industry.

2.2 IT Objectives

- To minimize dependence on IT personnel for mundane administrative tasks critical to task completion (regular reports, job monitoring, system restores, data manipulation), providing an initial end-user productivity boost.

- To improve the reliability and availability of core business systems and resources.

- To minimize total recurring IT cost structure by leveraging a corporate shared IT service center.

- To reposition IT resources as independent analysts, who are best qualified to drive continual process improvement and leverage IT investment dollars.

- To streamline and simplify information flows, including processing and delivery of "actionable" information.

2.3 Project Objectives

- To optimize internal processes. Continuous improvement in overhead efficiencies.

- To harmonize, where possible, business processes across product lines (including best practices).

- To prepare and "set the table" for eBusiness. To anticipate changing buying behaviors.

- KISS – To simplify and streamline current business practices.

- To capture "tribal knowledge" in a defined, documented, sustainable set of system-supported business processes.

- To build momentum for ERP implementation by securing buy-in from users & local management.

- To stay within given timeline and budget.

2.4 Process Automation Objectives

- To reduce the amount of organizational hand-offs & paper workaround processes in customer service/order entry by 70%.

- To reduce process cycle times (order entry, backorder scheduling, financial close, shipping) by 50%.

- To reduce overtime cost for basic transaction processing in targeted core processes by 50%.

- To enable better decision-quality information via integrated & timely information delivery.

3   Procedure

3.1 Implementation Approach

A business process-oriented implementation approach was chosen which is based on SAP's "ASAP" implementation methodology and enhanced and enriched by methods and tools used by IDS Scheer. Given the nature of American Meter Company's organizational structure, a phased implementation approach and not a "big bang" approach was adopted to implement the SAP R/3 standard software system. To make implementation as efficient and effective as possible, it was decided to create a template in a first step, which will then be rolled out to the respective business units and serve as the baseline for local implementations. The first phase of the project was therefore called Template Phase, which is followed by the roll-out phases to the five business units of Perfection Corporation (valves, raisers), Canadian Meter and North American Services Group, Residential Gas Meters, Commercial Gas Meters, and Automated Systems (remote gas meter reading devices). The complete project is scheduled for about two years.

The first phase, the **Template Phase**, lasted 4 months. The following illustration (figure 5) shows the main activities of this phase.

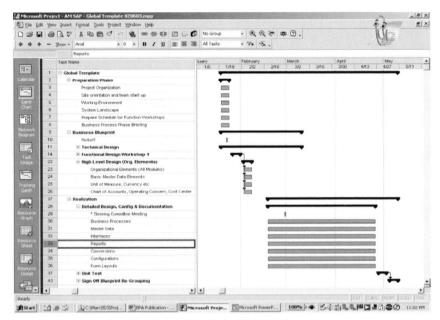

Fig. 5. Template Phase Master Schedule

The main objective of this phase was to design SAP-oriented common processes which can be rolled out to the business units. The starting points of this phase were the main enterprise processes, which were identified during a business process improvement project prior to this SAP implementation project. Examples are end-to-end processes for make-to-stock manufactured products, make-to-order manufactured configurable products, or the engineering services process. Based on these processes, a business process master list was developed, which showed on a detailed level the 120 business processes in scope while at the same time identifying potentially common processes. An excerpt of this list is depicted in the following illustration (table 1).

Table 1. Business Process Master List (Excerpt)

Level 1	Level 2	Level 3	1	2	3	3.1	4	5	6	7	8	9	10	11	GT	common	not common
	Procurement	MM Organization Structure	X	X	X	X	X	X	X	X	X	X	X		X	X	
		MRP Generated Purchases for Stock Material	X	X	X	X	X		X	X			X		X	X	
		Contract Purchases	X	X	X	X	X			X			X		X	X	
		Scheduling Agreement Purchases	X	X	X	X	X			X					X	X	
		Capital & Asset Purchases					X								X	X	
		Consignment Item Purchases	X		X	X									X	X	
		MRO Purchases	X		X	X					X	X	X		X	X	
		Expensed Item purchases	X	X	X	X	X	X	X	X	X	X	X	X	X	X	

Columns 1 to 11 and GT fall under the heading **Enterprise Processes**.

Please note: The numbers 1 to 11 represent the main enterprise business processes of American Meter Corporation.

For each process - which has been identified as either a common process or a process of strategic significance - a design document has been created. These design documents describe the business requirements, the areas of improvement, the potential impact on the organization, the process design (process flow), and the required customizing in SAP. These design documents were created by the project team, based on workshops held with participating parties from the business units. The final version of the design documents needed to be approved by American Meter's process owners. In addition to the maintenance of design documents, most of the processes were implemented on the development system and demonstrated to the business process owners and project team members in weekly Net Meeting sessions. This ensured that potential communication and understanding challenges were kept to a minimum.

At the end of the Template Phase, an SAP prototype with the designed business processes was demonstrated to the business process owners in a "go" or "no-go" decision workshop. In this workshop, all designed processes were demonstrated with prepared scripts as a basis. During the Template Phase, the business owners had seen business process fragments. In the final workshop, the end-to-end processes were demonstrated. This workshop was held in the first week of May 2003, and the decision makers gave the go-ahead to proceed with the first rollout.

The template was rolled out first to the Perfection business unit. This phase started immediately after the final workshop of the Template Phase. The Perfection business unit went live after six months, at the end of October 2003.

The main activities of this phase are depicted in the following graph (figure 6):

		May			June					July				August				September					October				November			
	Perfection Roll-Out																														
	Week	1	2	3	4	5	6	7	8	9	10	11	12	13	14	15	16	17	18	19	20	21	22	23	24	25	26	27	28	29
	Day of Month (Monday)	12	19	26	2	9	16	23	30	7	14	21	28	4	11	18	25	1	8	15	22	29	6	13	20	27	3	10	17	24
10	Finalize Process Design																													
20	Prepare Integration & Test Scripts																													
30	Super User Training																													
40	Integrationtest 1																													
50	Create Authorization Concept																													
60	Implement Authorization Concept																													
70	Data Conversion Programs Finalized																													
80	Create Cut-Over Plan																													
90	Test Load Master Data																													
100	Integrationtest 2 / Stress Test																													
110	Load Master Data																													
120	Execute Cut-Over																													
130	Live Start																													
140	End-User Training Preparation																													
150	End-User Training																													
160	After Live Start Support																													
170	Data Migration/Outputs/Interface																													
180	BW																													

Fig. 6. Perfection Rollout Schedule

In this rollout, the concept of a super-user was applied: a client process owner who leads the team of practitioners from the business unit. This allowed the customer to assume significant responsibility in order to shorten the implementation duration and limit reliance on external consultants. The primary responsibilities of this functional team leader were to 1) own and manage a complete and accurate set of function system requirements, 2) organize and mobilize the practitioners within their respective functions to define relevant business scenarios and test conditions,

3) coordinate end-user training, 4) define authorization roles, 5) coordinate the cleansing of data, and 6) learn as much as possible about the new system, in order to effectively provide 1st-level user support post-implementation.

3.2 Use of the ARIS Toolset and Reference Models

Although software reference models are available for the SAP software R/3 release 4.6c, these have not been used to a large extent in this project. The reason for this is that a comprehensive library of harmonized to-be business process maps created in the ARIS Toolset, developed and documented in the ARIS Toolset during the software selection process, already existed. These models were of great value to jump-start the Template Phase and to facilitate the workshops. They complemented the design documents in order to illustrate the process logics. From an efficiency standpoint, it was of great help that the business process design workshops had a point of departure and were not required to start from scratch.

4   Results

4.1 Results Achieved, Consistent with Defined Goals

Preliminary results indicate that the organization is well positioned to realize the improvements identified in the initial business case. Only the first of 5 rollout waves has been implemented to date, encompassing 3 of the 6 legal entities and 5 of the 13 plant locations. At press time, it is still too early to claim quantifiable benefits against the project business case, with only 4 weeks' experience on the live system, measurable improvements in process quality and cycle time were immediately visible. A sampling of process cycle time improvements, from the first month of experience with the new system automation, is illustrated in table 2:

Table 2. Initial Results, in the Area of Cycle Time Improvements

	Baseline Condition	Target	Actual	Improve-ment
MRP cycle time	8 Hr	1 Hr	<5 Min	100x
MRP Freq	1/Wk	5/Wk	2/Dy	12x
Customer In-quiry to Order Confirmation	2-4 Day	1 Day	2Min-1Day	4x+
Cumulative Manufacturing Lead Time	3-5 Weeks	2 Weeks	1-3 Weeks	2x+
Financial Close	6 Days	2 Days	3 Days	2x

4.1.1 Project focus helped to yield desired results

A clear definition of "to-be" processes (ARIS models, catalogued improvement potentials, discrete savings targets) helped the project maintain a tight focus on the "critical few" process changes (those that must be done right the first time) while not wasting valuable time and energy on the "trivial many" automation opportunities of a flexible IT solution such as the one provided by SAP.

4.1.2 Speed (Cycle Time) of Process Execution is Key to Management Flexibility

The automated processes, taken together, enabled a rapid, transparent, visible and integrated information flow across the various functions within the enterprise. The result is an organizational *speed*, which has literally created new flexibility and management decision-making prerogatives; this is simply because before the processes were automated, the right information never got in the hands of people who could capitalize on it, or when it did, the information was too stale to act on.

4.1.3 Strong and Experienced Project Team is Invaluable

The project was able to stay on schedule and under budget throughout the project lifecycle. While it is still early in the ROI timeline, the improvements generated are also consistent with project business case targets. Primarily, this is the direct result of having an experienced project team who, in addition to team lead responsibilities in several SAP implementations, each had line responsibilities in their respective functions prior to becoming involved with SAP software. As a result, the team instinctively knew where, when and how to fill in the process integration gaps and influence adopted best practices.

4.1.4 Workforce Approaching "Tipping Point"

The workforce is becoming accustomed with the new tools and processes, which, like any major change, takes several repetitions in a live environment to develop competence and confidence. We are now starting to see innovative improvement opportunities suggested by the system end-users as to where we can better leverage the substantial IT investment. This is by far the most potent expected outcome of the project, and it is happening earlier than anticipated.

4.1.5 "Birds of a Feather" Communities Emerged

In a highly distributed organization like the American Meter group of companies, one of the side effects is inadequate communication between practitioners in a given profession (buyers, accountants, customer service representatives, IT analysts). Many of the people in these "like communities" spend considerable energy solving very similar problems for their respective divisions, but don't have the time, inclination or relationship to tap into the collective intelligence throughout the enterprise. One of the outcomes of this project has been the evolution of deeper relationships among these "birds-of-a-feather" communities, to share lessons learned and solicit experiential learning regarding current problems.

5   Lessons Learned

5.1 Heavily Involve "Practitioner" Level Personnel

Involving the end-user, who knows how the process is executed on a day-to-day basis (as opposed to how it should be executed), is of paramount importance. This person knows all the exception conditions, and these should be tested against the new/automated process to ensure that the solution implemented is robust. Since the "devil is in the details", an appointed process owner or team lead who isn't also a de facto process expert may not know the devil's every haunt.

5.2 Resist the Temptation to Utilize any and all Automation Provided by the new System

Process change must be managed as a function of the cultural tolerance for change within the organization. There will be "early adopters", who will push to do more and be quicker than the organization can absorb. In the end, and especially where there is a high degree of functional integration, the organizational effectiveness as a whole is only as strong as its weakest link. As the "critical mass" becomes accustomed to the initial integration and automation, more can be added incrementally relatively easily and actually increases the traction from the initial effort. Trying to implement more than the "critical mass" can absorb only creates a fracture in the process integration, and this impedes the ability to successfully realize initial improvements.

Business Process Automation: Automating and Monitoring the Mortgage Process

Yvonne Cook
American Business Financial Services, Inc.

Trevor Naidoo
IDS Scheer, Inc.

Summary

This case study illustrates the benefits gained from implementing the full lifecycle of BPM, i.e. from Process Design to Process Automation to Process monitoring. ABFS has implemented the full lifecycle for their Loan Origination Process and gained a 15% productivity increase within the first 3 months of implementation.

Key Words

Workflow, Process Performance Management, Loan Process, Increased Productivity, Improved Efficiency

1   Abstract

This chapter will describe how American Business Financial Services, Inc. (ABFS), embarked on business process excellence by implementing a workflow system and business process performance management system. In order to increase productivity in their loan origination process, ABFS has automated it. In order to standardize the process and ensure that the loan origination process is executed in a consistent manner, a workflow solution is the most appropriate solution. The workflow solution delivers the greatest benefit when combined with a process monitoring application to aid in the effective management and optimization of the process.

2   Background

2.1 Company Profile

American Business Financial Services, Inc., is a financial services holding company operating predominantly in the eastern and central portions of the United States. The mission of ABFS and its subsidiaries – American Business Credit, Inc., HomeAmerican Credit, Inc. d/b/a Upland Mortgage, and American Business Mortgage Services, Inc., – is to make loans, secured by real estate, to consumers and small businesses who either do not qualify for or do not wish to deal with banks and other traditional lenders to meet their borrowing needs.

ABFS pursues its mission by offering its services through a broad range of distribution channels that include mail, telephone, branch offices, the Internet, mortgage brokers, and bank partners. ABFS' staff is trained to offer customers loan products that best meet their needs in a consistent and cost-effective manner. ABFS currently has more than 700 employees.

3   Business Drivers

ABFS handles a high volume of mortgage loans. To increase the productivity of the employees and potentially process more loans with the same level of resources, ABFS decided to automate the process using a workflow engine. Before automating the process, ABFS had to understand the process, including its inefficiencies.

The key business drivers were as follows:

3.1 Increasing Monthly Loan Closings

In order to achieve this, it was necessary to overcome the operations bottlenecks to increase throughput.

3.2 Enhancing Employee Productivity

With the economic challenges faced today, it is imperative that current resources be used effectively and efficiently. This initiative has helped ABFS accomplish that. When dealing with high loan volume, it is important to identify those loans that have higher priority and assign the resources to these loans as necessary. ABFS also identified non-productive steps with the purpose of eliminating these steps to make the end-to-end process more efficient.

3.3 Management Controls

As the process becomes more efficient and effective via automation, it is important for the management to be able to check up on process performance. Managers need to have a view of resource allocation and of the status of processes along the way. In order to be proactive, managers need to have information that allows them to make decisions to prevent delays in a proactive manner. With this information at their fingertips, managers can become coaches instead of putting out fires.

These business drivers led ABFS to conclude that it needed to implement a workflow system and a process performance system.

4   Situation Analysis Prior to Project

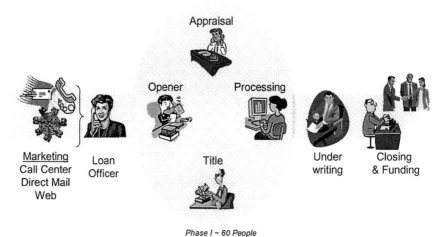

Phase I ~ 60 People

Fig. 1. Basic Loan Origination Process

4.1 Process Challenges

- "Multi Media"
  The environment offers many openings for inefficiency, one possible source of inefficiency being the multitude of media used. ABFS currently uses a loan origination system, faxes, e-mail, voicemail, paper, paper and more paper.

- Multi-department process flow
  This process involves many different departments, with information flowing between them. This leads to many handoffs and as a result may lead to many inefficiencies.

- Production pressures
  The pressure is to sell, sell, sell and close, close, close, and as a result the environment is more reactive than proactive.

- Process changes and user training
  Since most of the process is manual, there is some risk of not having a repeatable process. In addition, employee turnover, may make it difficult to ensure that new employees execute the process in a standard and efficient way.

4.2 Solution Approach

The project approach was to deploy the solution to a pilot group who could validate the desired business outcomes. The initial user base included 35 loan processors, 10 appraisal reps, 3 title reps, 10 loan openers and associated management. Once this group achieved increased production goals and demonstrated success, the solution could then be rolled out to the remainder of the company.

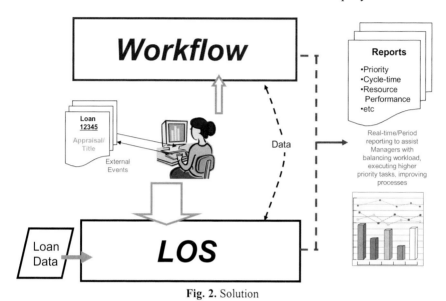

Fig. 2. Solution

4.3 The Proposed Solution Concept

The solution illustrated above best describes ABFS' approach. The workflow system was put in place in conjunction with ABFS' Loan Origination System. Both these systems pass data on to a process performance management system to provide management and controlling reports and information. To support this solution, ABFS had to choose software products to match system requirements.

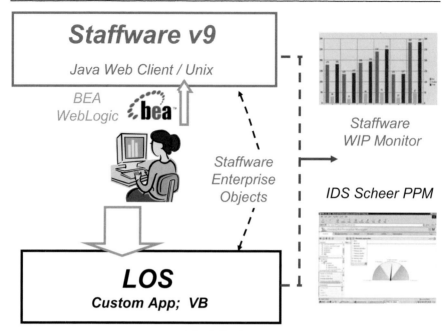

Fig. 3. Products

4.4 The Software Products

Following a comprehensive evaluation of various software products for the automation of its Loan Origination process, ABFS chose Staffware as its workflow engine and Process Performance Manager (PPM) from IDS Scheer as its process monitoring tool. While the workflow engine provided ABFS with monitoring capability, this was not sufficient for management decisions using historical data. PPM provided us with the capability to look for trends and evaluate its process KPIs by different dimensions. PPM provided Process Intelligence.

5   Future Workflow Design

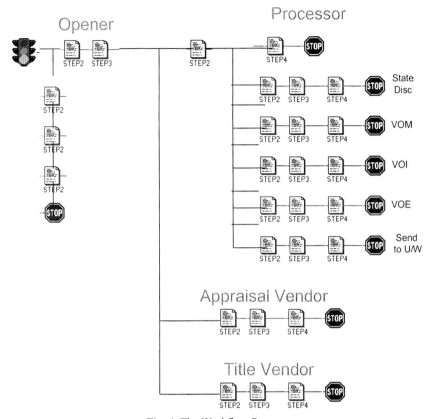

Fig. 4. The Workflow Process

After optimizing the current process, ABFS implemented the optimized process in the Staffware Workflow engine. The process shown above is the automated process that was implemented in Staffware and monitored using Process Performance Manager.

6   Management Tools

The workflow engine allows visibility into the current workload and the ability to track the status of process instances. With this tool, managers can monitor the work in process (WIP). Process instances can be tracked and reassigned if needed.

This feature allows managers to proactively monitor system performance and balance the workload if resources are overutilized.

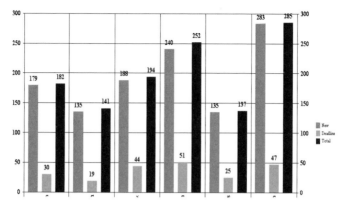

Fig. 5. Sample Chart – Workflow Engine

While it is important to manage the current workload, it is also important to analyze past performance for trends and process intelligence. The IDS Scheer Process Performance Manager tool gave ABFS the capability to analyze the past performance of its critical process KPIs (Key Performance Indicators). This historical data can also be analyzed for specific dimensions, e.g. selecting for loan type.

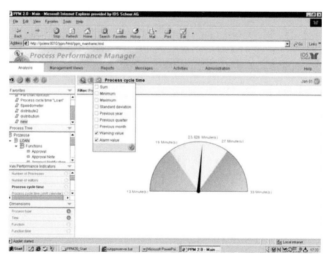

Fig. 6. Sample Chart – PPM (Process Performance Manager)

With tools to manage the daily activities and tools to proactively analyze process trends, managing ABFS' processes becomes easier.

7   Key Results

The workflow system has been in production for over a year. Within the first 3 months, employee productivity increased by more than 15%. The new user learning curve was reduced significantly. New users could be put out onto the floor much earlier thanks to process-oriented training and the tools to enforce a standard process.

8   Conclusion

After this initiative, ABFS strongly believes in the concepts of business process management. ABFS has seen real results in regard to benefits in productivity and it wants more. This approach has been successful but ABFS has learned some lessons along the way that will allow it to derive even more benefit in the future. ABFS' next step is to fine-tune its approach and move ahead.

8.1 Sample Job Aids

Below are sample job aids that ABFS used to help the end users identify with the terminology used by the system. The job aids put the system terminology into business terms that the end users use on a daily basis.

This table is for *Process Level* KPI's which is analagous to *Loan Level* KPI's		
Original KPI Name	Upland KPI Name	What it really means / What it really measures
Number of Processes	Number of Loans	Number of Loans in the workflow system (Since Sep 11, 2002)
Number Of Processors	Number of Users	Number of different people working the loan case (e.g., Processors, DSA, Vendors/Reps, Auto-users);
Process Cycle Time	Loan Time in WIP	Current/Total elapsed time active in Workflow system
Process Cycle Time (Shift)	Loan Time in WIP (Work Days)	Current/Total elapsed time active in Workflow system (Working Days only)
Process Frequency	Loan-case starts per day	Average number of loans per day being started in Workflow system; The User can change units to Sec/Min/Hr/Day/Month/Qtr/Year
Processing Frequency	Work Items per Loan-Case	Average number of Workflow steps being executed per loan case
TIP Bias Delay	Start Case-to-Processing Time	Elapsed time from Start of Loan-case to when Processor receives "Review File" workflow item in their work queue
TIP Cycle Time	Processor Work Time	Elapsed time from when Processor receives "Review File" Step to when the Workflow loan-case is terminated
TIP Cycle Time (Shift)	Processor Work Time (Work Days)	Same as WF-TIP Cycle Time using only Working Days

Fig. 7. User Cheat Sheet I

This table is for **Function Level** KPI's which is analagous to **Activity/Task level** KPI's		
Original KPI Name	**Upland KPI Name**	**What it really means / What it really measures**
Cycle Time	Work Item Time	Total time a work item remains in a user's work queue; the time from when assigned to User to when released
Cycle Time (Shift)	Work Item Time (Work Days)	Total time a work item remains in a user's work queue (Working Days Only)
Function Frequency	Completed Work Items per Day	The average number of times work item has been completed per day (PPM only acknowledges items that have been completed)
Number Of Functions	Total Work Items	The total number of work items within selected sample; Could be time, group, users, …
Cycle Span	Cycle Span	New; Average time difference between latest end time of a work step and earliest end time of preceeding functions.
Cycle Span (Shift)	Cycle Span (Work Days)	New; Same as above but using Work days only
Processing Time	Work Item Work Time	New; Analagous/Identical to Cycle time for Upland WF
Processing Time (Shift)	Work Item Work Time (Shift)	New; Same as above except work days only

Fig. 8. User Cheat Sheet II

Excellence in Vehicle Financing

Peter Westermann
DC Bank AG

Frank Gahse
IDS Scheer AG

Summary

DaimlerChrysler Bank invested into a Business Process Automation solution for their finance request process. The bank then decided to testcase ARIS Process Performance Manager to improve and manage the "Degree of Business Process Automation", boosting response times to customers, thus increasing customer satisfaction, "Hit Rates" and reducing costs due to fewer manual interactions.

Key Words

Process Performance Management, Key Performance Indicator, Straight Through Processing, Service Level, Customer Facing Business Process, Return on IT Investment

1   Initial Situation

DaimlerChrysler Bank is a leading Auto-Bank in Europe and has been a full-service bank since summer 2002. We are the financial services company of DaimlerChrysler Services in Germany. With our products, we are ensuring more mobility, a wider range of financial opportunities and financial security to private and commercial customers.

Our offer includes financing, leasing, insurances and fleet management for the brands Mercedes-Benz, smart, Chrysler, Jeep and Setra. Moreover, we offer daily cash accounts, fixed-rate investment accounts, savings plans and the DaimlerChrysler Card to private customers. RoadMiles is an additional revenue bonus program for all direct bank products. Exclusively for Mercedes drivers, there is the MercedesCard offered by Mercedes-Benz.

DaimlerChrysler Bank is striving for Business Process Excellence to ensure their customers select DaimlerChrysler Bank as supplier of choice. These are two slogans DaimlerChrysler Bank advertizes in Germany which underline the promise of process excellence: "The Fascination for a new car shouldn't stop with its financing" and "The focus point is always the customer".

DaimlerChrysler Bank customers wish their mobility dreams to be fulfilled and their financial mobility to be ensured. To quickly react towards customer needs, every dealer needs fast response on vehicle finance requests. This enables the dealer to present different options and ultimately win business. In Fleet Management, which is part of DC Bank, perfect service levels and operational excellence are key to success in a highly competitive market. Therefore the customer-facing business processes need to be fast and reliable. Business Process Excellence is mandatory. This can be achieved by implementing well designed business processes with flexible application systems. An excellent process can only be delivered upon continuous monitoring. If weaknesses are detected, an improvement process will automatically be initiated. Process Performance Management (PPM) strives to continuously improve business processes.

PPM is not only a paradigm but a software tool from IDS Scheer (IDS) as part of the ARIS process platform. To verify PPM both as paradigm and tool, DC Bank decided to testcase the automated vehicle financing process called Easyline Process. This testcase serves as the first of two phases, which delivers approximately two thirds of the complete results with one third of the total effort. The Easyline Process was recently implemented with an application system independent process automation layer. For this layer DC Bank selected an Enterprise Application Integration (EAI) approach, which is implemented with BusinessWare from Vitria. The return of this investment into Business Process Automation needs to be measured and insured. Within corporate controlling, a list of mostly financial Key Performance Indicators (KPI's) already get measured either manually or automatically. Some KPI's were newly introduced, such as *level of automation.* Process

Performance Management has to measure all business process-related KPI's. More importantly, it has to graphically visualize the business process instances, which were the root for the cause of a manual interference.

Consequently, the expected value was to detect and better understand the potentials for improvement in the automated Easyline Process. DC Bank customers and dealers will benefit from the improved business processes with faster response times. DC Bank expects improvement in customer satisfaction, lower costs, improved dealer relationship and the return on the investment into Business Process Automation.

2   Business Requirements

2.1 Strategic Goals

To define PPM requirements, it is recommended to start with the strategic goals or project goals to ensure that meeting the PPM requirements really improves business by achieving those goals. The Strategic goals were: improving customer-facing processes and accelerating return on the Easyline investments by reducing manual interaction.

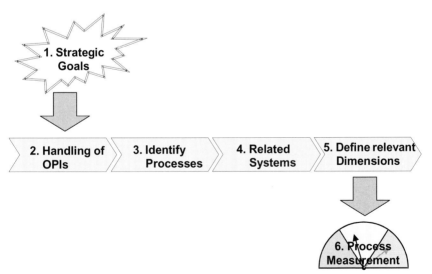

Fig. 1. Defining PPM Business Requirements at DC Bank

The project goals for phase 1 of the phased PPM implementation were defined as follows:

1. Depicting the technically most useful implementation path (beneficial for future roll outs).

2. Acquiring a good understanding for the whole PPM approach from a management perspective.

3. Receiving better backup data for the cost/ benefit case.

4. Understanding potential extensions of the implemented PPM solution, e.g. by process mining, activity-based costing, process design.

5. Identifying weaknesses of the approach taken and lessons learned.

2.2 Defining Operational Performance Indicators

In order to measure goal achievement, a set of Operational Performance Indicators (OPI is a DC Bank term) needs to be defined and target values set. OPI's are dynamic and process-related indicators versus static and more financial-oriented indicators. For the project, we decided on a two-phased approach, where the higher prioritized OPI's with a medium effort get implemented first. During the second phase, OPI's with lower priority or with higher effort will also be implemented. The following chart shows sample OPI's with explanation and definition as laid out by DC Banks Process Controlling Department.

Table 1. Definition of Operational Performance Indicators for Phase 1

Operational Performance Indicator	Definition	Classification
Easyline Utilization Rate: How many proposals are done made via Easyline?	Number of incoming Easyline proposals ---------------------------------- Number of total incoming proposals	Quality, Efficiency
Manual Interruption Rate: How many Easyline proposals are stuck in a worklist? Process from transfer of the proposal to start the credit check (trigger the scoring). Importance to identify all the interrupted workflows and the special reasons for manual intervention.	Number. of incoming and transferred Easyline proposals with manual interruption ---------------------------------- Number of total incoming and transferred Easyline proposals	Quality
Proposal Productivity Factor: How many proposals are handled by the related personnel? To identify productivity of sales staff in the area of proposal handling (until credit check).	Number of incoming and transferred Easyline proposals ---------------------------------- Number of total staff in "VU-process"	Productivity

Table 1. (continued)

Operational Performance Indicator	Definition	Classification
Level of automation: How many Easyline proposals were handled automatically? To identify degree of automation of the proposal management process.	Number of auto-decided proposals -------------------------------- Number of total incoming proposals	Efficiency
Score result rate: How many proposals are in a special scoring range? To identify the risk of special proposal constellation / customer groups/object types.	Number of scored proposals with special score result -------------------------------- Number of total incoming and transferred Easyline proposals	Risk
Cycle time of proposal management process (several time stamps): What is the average cycle time of an end to end Easyline proposal respectively partial processes?	Cycle time (total; data transfer and proposal processing; credit decision; communication) -------------------------------- Incoming and transferred Easyline proposal	Efficiency, Service Level
Proposal change rate/ circulating rate: How many Easyline proposals are changed after communicating the decision (per new incoming proposal)?	Number of changed Easyline proposals after communication -------------------------------- Number of total incoming and transferred Easyline proposals	Quality, Efficiency

The OPI's level of automation and Cycle Time became mandatory business requirement for Phase 1 of the PPM implementation.

2.3 Easyline Process Description

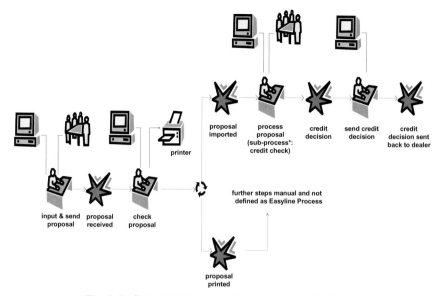

Fig. 2. Defining PPM Business Requirements at DC Bank

This is how the "Happy Path" of the Easyline Process looks: A prospect in the dealer's showroom is ready to purchase his desired vehicle, a CLK430. The dealer cannot sign the contract unless the financial contract is cleared. Therefore the dealer collects the required data from his prospect and sends the (vehicle finance) proposal electronically to DC Bank. The input data from the dealer are complete and in the correct format. Thus the credit check with the scoring process continues automatically and clears successfully. The positive credit decision is sent back to the dealer. This is where the Easyline Process finishes. The dealer had to wait less than 1 minute for the positive credit decision. His prospect in the showroom feels well serviced and signs the contract for his desired CLK 430. Now, after the vehicle has been ordered – which implicitly means that the financial terms are signed off – the vehicle assembly can be planned at the relevant DaimlerChrysler plant.

Unfortunately, the Easyline Process does not always follow the "Happy Path". Sometimes the input data from the dealer are not complete and have to be revised by the dealer. Either that or they might be complete though don't meet all criteria for automatic processing by Easyline. This may be because the proposal is customized for a commercial customer, or the payment terms are not on a monthly basis. Even if the proposal is processed by Easyline, the credit check can fail, e.g. when the customer is known but not credible or if the response from the credit agency is not perfect. In such cases, DC Bank may need additional information from the dealer respectively the prospect or they escalate the case to their support center. Finally, once the dealer presents the proposal to the prospect, the prospect might want to test a different financing alternative or postpone the deal.

2.4 Defining OPI Dimensions

Dimensions are views of the OPI's and are maintained consistently. When a credit analyst or a business analyst detects an anomaly on the OPI level, the only way to get closer to the root cause is to drill down into various dimensions of the OPI. Assuming the goal for straight-through-processing measured by the OPI, "Automated Decisioning Rate" is defined as 80%, if the actual OPI was 60%, all that the credit analyst knows is that the degree of automation is far below plan. This conclusion, however, is not decision supporting. Instead, if we can consistently track the reasons why Easyline rejects some proposals, we will be able to pinpoint potentials for improvement. Knowing more about the rejection reasons will support managers to take better decisions.

The table below depicts a number of dimensions for the OPIs from 2.1.

Table 2. Definition of OPI Dimensions for Phase 1

Dimension	Dimension Values	Priority for Phase 1
Financial product/contract type	Leasing, financing standard, contracts with campaigns (campaign no.), ...	Medium
Brand	Mercedes-Benz, Chrysler, smart, ...	Medium
Condition of vehicle	new, used	Medium
Object type	Passenger car, van, truck, other	Medium
Customer segment and industry)	Private, commercial, and industry	High
Business line (only relevant for retail)	Retail, charter way, fleet management, banking, wholesale, ...	Medium
Internal organization	Region, sales team, operational team ranking should be possible	High
External organization	Dealership, salesmen, ranking should be possible	High
Time period	Daily, weekly, monthly, yearly	High

3   Architecture of the Desired Solution

To extract process oriented information of every single Easyline process instance, ARIS PPM utilizes sensors. The extracted information includes all attributes necessary to represent the OPIs from the business requirements. An efficient tactic is to extract only those data which are required for the OPIs in order to avoid useless data volume. To understand the process logic of one process instance, ARIS PPM needs to retrieve a unique identifier for a business process instance. For every single step in the process, PPM tracks an identifier for that step along with a time stamp. The time stamp is the key information for PPM to understand the sequencing of the steps within an end-to-end process instance. Thus, ARIS PPM extracts unstructured information and creates business processes. The standard extraction format is xml. These business process instances get stored into a data base which could be called a process warehouse. For Easyline, roughly 10,000-20,000 instances per month are stored in the process warehouse. PPM calculates process-oriented OPIs and categorizes them by dimensions.

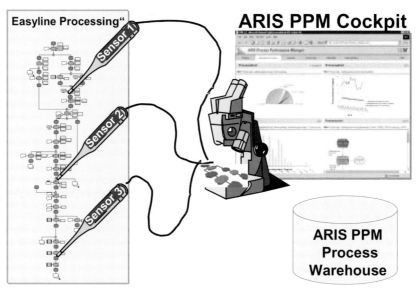

Fig. 3. ARIS PPM Data Extraction and Mapping

OLAP-type technologies query in the process warehouse. The results can be presented with more than 30 different business charts. Normally, the sensors are set into critical process areas such as organizational hand-offs or system interfaces. At DC Bank, the data extraction was much easier to implement. This was due to the Process Automation layer EAI (Enterprise Application Integration). DC Bank opted for the product suite BusinessWare from Vitria as Process Automation layer. Vitria collects the business process information and controls the operative flow. BusinessWare hands over all relevant information for monitoring to ARIS PPM. [cf. Kühl 2003]

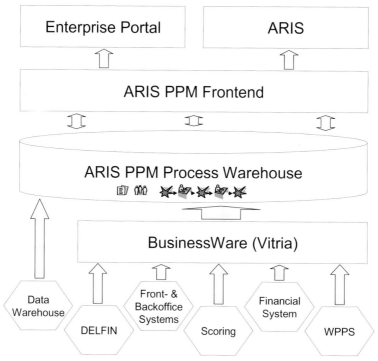

Fig. 4. ARIS PPM Architecture at DCB

The Process Performance Management architecture [IDS Scheer AG 2002.] needs to support the entire business process lifecycle. As-is business process instances can be transferred to ARIS Toolset. Weaknesses in the as-is processes should be communicated and discussed to continuously improve process design. ARIS PPM process instances can be simulated in ARIS Toolset to perform "what-if" scenarios. An enterprise portal might be used to integrate various corporate performance reporting.

4   Implementation Path

4.1 A Phased Approach

The implementation of PPM for the Easyline Process followed a two-phase approach with

- Phase 1 delivering two thirds of the desired solution with one third of the total project effort. This could be achieved as only requirements with low effort were defined for Phase 1, thus taking advantage of PPM standard deliverables. After Phase 1, DC Bank had to decide if they wanted to cancel the license contract. Thus Phase 1 allows for tangible results quickly, at the same time lowering the risk for the strategic purchase decision. Also the total cost of ownership and the organizational implications could be better understood. The prototype was a much better means of communicating and selling the expected benefits internally at DC Bank than only communicating wishes and hopes. As PPM is a paradigm shift into process-oriented management, the first phase very effectively visualized the new paradigm.

- Phase 2 will complete the implementation of the business requirements mainly by the more time-consuming activities e.g. customer specific KPIs, dimensions, reports, management views or alerts.

The chart below shows the implementation path for Phase 1, customized from the recommended ARIS PPM standard implementation path. DC Bank followed the sequence of activities but by-passed the "Adapter Creation" as they took advantage of the already existing BusinessWare export format. The main activities are described in this chapter.

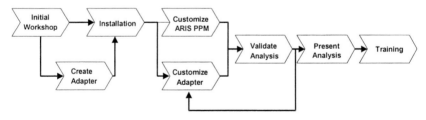

Fig. 5. Chart X: ARIS PPM Implementation Path Phase 1

4.2 Project Roles

The major contributors to the project along with their main tasks are described in the table below:

Table 3. Project Roles and Their Contributions

Role	Contribution
IT: Manager Business Architecture	As owner of the Vitria EAI platform, he confirms decisions on IT platforms as well as data extraction
	Approves data access for ARIS PPM to source systems
IT: Business Architect	Is well-informed on business requirements and provides data extracts for ARIS PPM import.
Business Analyst/Process Controller	Defines business requirements
	Owns and manages project
Business Owner Easyline Process	Sponsors and provides feedback
IDS Scheer Consultant	Supports in project management
	ARIS PPM implementation according to business requirements
	Provides guidance and education

4.3 Initial Workshop

The initial workshop took one day and included all roles involved in Phase 1 of the project. Goal of the initial workshop was first of all to acquire a common understanding of the Easyline requirements. Then, the best implementation scenario was discussed. It was decided to focus on the data extraction from Vitrias BusinessWare into IDS Scheers ARIS PPM. The implementation path was defined and scheduled along with the expected delivery.

4.4 Data Mapping

Four different parties were involved in the data extraction:

DC Bank IT and Business Analysis as well as Vitria for the export from BusinessWare and IDS Scheer for the import into ARIS PPM. After some trials, DC Bank IT, IDS Scheer and Vitria decided to use a standard BusinessWare export-format from BusinessWare into ARIS PPM. DC Bank IT architects were already well trained and experienced with BusinessWare, so they could run and adapt the export file for PPM themselves. After some learning, the data export was suitable to cover the Phase 1 requirements.

DC Bank's data mapping was considered successful by IDS Scheer after the provided export file had carried all required data and all data had been allocated to single processes instances. Roughly 30,000 Easyline process instance samples were exported from Vitria into ARIS PPM, covering finance request process samples from the past three months.

4.5 ARIS PPM Customizing

Customizing includes all activities needed to extend standard PPM. These activities consist of implementing a process type with all relevant process fragments, OPI's, dimensions, reports, management views and alerts to meet the project specific requirements. At DC Bank, the entire PPM customizing was performed by one dedicated IDS Scheer consultant, which provides for fast results. The customizing skills will be transferred to DC Bank during the ARIS PPM rollout. Some OPI's such as cycle time could easily be implemented by customizing existing standard PPM OPI's. Other OPI's, such as "Level of Automation", required more customizing. The definition of this OPI is not very complex. It is mainly how many proposals could be handled automatically, which means we have to divide the number of credit decisions by the number of proposals. The number of credit decisions was a specific attribute in the extracted process instances and can be calculated easily by ARIS PPM. However, the number of proposals is not available in the source data or in the source systems. As workaround, we took data which allowed us to calculate the number of proposals entering the Easyline Process and the number of proposals being printed. Adding both numbers results in the number of proposals.

4.5 Go Live/Training

The customizing of ARIS PPM was mostly done remotely. All contributors and stakeholders participated in the presentation of the results. For those who knew PPM, it was satisfying to see the fruits of their work by

- Technically meeting the requirements

- Being confronted with analysis results, which were process-oriented and new

For those who had not been exposed to ARIS PPM before, it was a new experience to see DC Bank's process performance, now capable to dig into the causing process instances. After the presentation, the key users were coached in the base functionality of PPM and how to analyze the existing process data. The coaching was to take one day to ensure that the user can be successful during the test phase. This is in the best interest of both parties. In the Phase "Go Live" we will set PPM operative and establish continuous data extraction.

4.6 Testing

Testing was done by DC Bank over a period of two months after training on ARIS PPM with Easyline data. The testing included:

Table 4. ARIS PPM Validation Criteria and Results

Item	Result
Analysis capability	All the analysis types, such as trend analysis, slicing and dicing and root cause analysis, were beyond expectation. Process Mining was not yet a requirement. Details are described in chapter 5.
Validating correctness of OPI values	OPI values measured by ARIS PPM were compared with manually calculated OPIs or existing OPI reports. All OPI matched.
Verify look and feel	Various groups within DC Bank from the business side, business analysis and IT Architecture were very pleased and see the graphical user interface as a contributor for future success.
System Performance	The various contributors to performance had to be analyzed. Optimizing standard Oracle technology was key to high performance review on a small scale physical server. Training is again critical, as users need to understand, what type of analysis are demanding on the system performance e.g. analysis of three OPI's with no filter on process types on a function level.
Verifying hardware requirements for future rollout	ForPhase 1, ARIS PPM server was implemented on an average desktop PC and worked well. To run ARIS PPM operatively for Easyline as well as future processes, sufficiently sized hardware will be ordered, which can grow for another ten or more process types within the next two years and must then be scalable withthen state of the art better and cheaper storage.
Verifying system operations requirements for future rollout	As part of DC Bank system operations strategy, the IT Architects defined the appropriate system operations plan for ARIS PPM by ensuring: backup/restore functionality, system monitoring and availability, archiving concept, clustering capability and system scalability
Validating, roles and responsibilities for future rollout	Upon first experience with ARIS PPM, roles had to be defined according to DC Bank policy ■ who carries on core ARIS PPM responsibility ■ line responsibility in the business areas ■ process controlling and system operations responsibility.

4.7. Plan Phase 2 Implementation

After DC Bank went through the test phase, business requirements were first outlined internally in a workshop categorized by

- Additional OPI's   - Additional Dimensions

- Process Structure   - RIS PPM tool functionality

and prioritized the requirements with high/middle/low.

The result of the internal workshop was then verified with IDS Scheer and led to an implementation plan covering Business Concept and IT Concept along with detailed activities, roles, deliverables and milestones. DC Bank defined the complete Easyline implementation as template for future ARIS PPM implementations. The requirements were therefore well thought through, not only for the Easyline requirements but also to be reusable as standards template.

5   Potential Analysis Path

Reporting, analysis, simulation, optimization and control are the key potentials and focus in working with ARIS PPM. The reporting capability is not only static but includes dynamic trend analysis, cross-organizational comparisons such as rankings and a flexible depiction of essential indicators.

The analyst can change contributing process parameter as "what-if" scenarios via simulation to estimate the impact on the relevant OPI's. The derived conclusions serve as foundation to define the potentials for improvement and to break down the concrete activities for realizing the suggested process improvement.

Permanent measuring in the context of corporate audit and distinct process reviews makes the efficiency of the improvement activities transparent, thus enabling a continuous improvement process.

The major advantage DC Bank sees in utilizing ARIS PPM is the analysis capability deep into the desired business processes. Major goal was to provide the required transparency which allows the key influencing factors to be identified and process weaknesses to be clearly detected.

The root-cause analysis follows the principle:

- WHAT exactly happened?
- HOW did it happen?
- WHY did it happen?

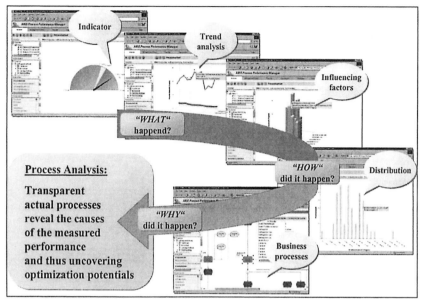

Fig. 6. Process Analysis: 5 Steps From Indicator to Process Instance

The WHAT as first step in the analysis provides a quick overview of the relevant OPI values. The HOW leverages PPM as success control for the process owner, and the WHY finally represents the foundation for identifying the potentials for improvement for the business area responsible.

This analysis sequence will be validated in the ARIS PPM business case for DC Banks Easyline Process.

5.1 Background

The Finance Request Process is on the critical success path in managing leasing- and finance contracts. The dealer and the end-customer expect a fast release process. The internal quality has to sustain highest standards and the respective credit risk always has to be validated and managed. Most importantly, the profitability of every single contract is viewed as the bottom line. Because of this complexity, the key OPI's are essential to manage and control business.

5.2 Organizational Responsibility

As depicted in the chart below, the process improvement cycle has a certain complexity. This is why the operational responsibilities become a critical success factor. A paradigm shift from a pure function-oriented to a process-oriented structure is required to implement continuous process improvement. This includes not only PPM operations but also the management and control of the end-to-end business process in the context of a continuous improvement cycle:

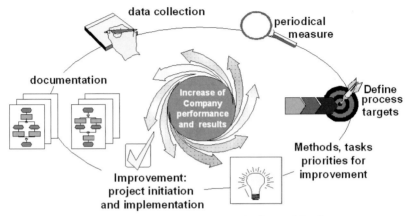

Fig. 7. Process Improvement Cycle at DC Bank

The organizational responsibility will be composed as follows:

1. Management/Controlling

- Defining the methodological foundation (calculating OPI's, dimensions, business charts, reports, management views e.g.)

- Setting the key OPI's and their target values with the operative business areas

- Translating the OPI's into a corporate target system

- Frequent reporting of the OPI's

- Root-cause analysis of deviations in the sense of cockpit reporting

- Initiating improvement activities

2. Operations (Process Owner)

- Responsible for the end-to-end business process as process owner

- Initiating and implementing improvement activities

- Controlling success and effectiveness of improvement activities

- Serving as "key accounter" for all operative business areas

3. Operative Business Areas

- Responsible for operative process management

- Communicating potentials for improvement

- Detailed business process analysis by all process contributors

There are many potential roadblocks to continuous process improvement. The described concept can succeed only if the individual tasks are well synchronized, prioritized towards their goals and managed as part of an iterative process.

This process will be described with the business case of the Easyline Process.

5.3 Speedometer and Assessment Diagram

For Upper Management or for the Controlling Department the key OPI's are depicted in a cockpit format to represent the key findings. Few business charts are necessary to provide this transparency. For the Easyline Process, two key OPI's were defined:

1. The level of (business process) automation
   The level of automation is a key indicator for the efficiency of the process. The representation as bar diagram was considered sufficient. The "automated decisioning rate" can be viewed directly in the business chart and compared with its target value.

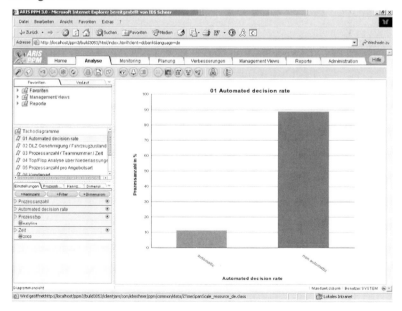

Fig. 8. Representation of Automated Decision Rate

2. Cycle Time

How long does the finance request process take from request entry to confirmation at the point of sale? This OPI is not only an indicator for process efficiency but also for achieving an agreed service level with the dealer, at the same time meeting the expectations of the end-customer. The management cockpit represents the current status of different partial cycle times with traffic-light color coding. These key OPIs can be provided and communicated via various reporting formats such as intranet, e-mail, as paper document or directly inside ARIS PPM.

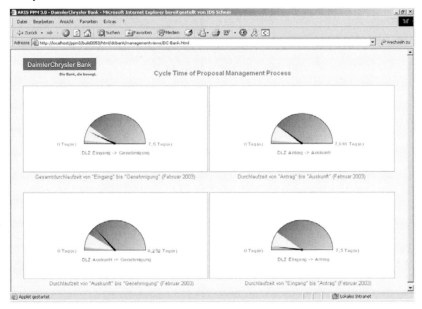

Fig. 9. Representation of Cycle Time Cockpit

5.4 Drill Down Into Dimensions

To provide the process owner level with the right leverage to manage and control his business process, more detailed information is required. For the tasks of the process owner, the OPI's will be sliced and diced into various dimensions. If the process owner wants to monitor predefined analysis, a number of PPM-favorites are set, similarly to internet bookmarks. In case of the OPI Level of Automation, the process owner could also see all non-automated decisions in further granularity. The most frequent reason for interruptions might be the different way of processing private versus business customers. To find out the significance, the OPI should be differentiated into the dimension Customer Segment.

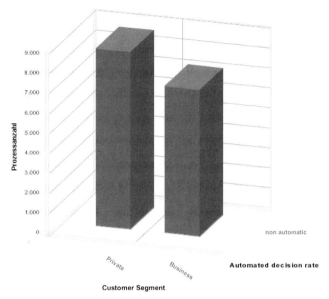

Fig. 10. Representation of Non-Automated Decisions per Customer Segment

The root-cause analysis could be detailed filtering the different product lines (the dimension is called "Object Type") such as cars, trucks. Once this transparency is provided per product line, the next analysis step might be to differentiate per dimension Time and per Operating Business Unit. The result will represent in which period and in which business unit the cycle time was off-target respectively into which direction we foresee trends of improvement or decrease.

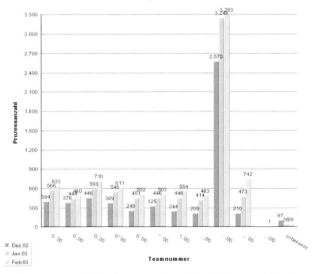

Fig. 11. Non-Automated Decisions per Operational Business Unit Over Time

Thus the analysis is mature enough that significant anomalies get discovered. Consequently, supporting activities with the operational business units can now be initiated.

5.5 Drill Down Into Process Instances

Critical areas for the operational business units will be analyzed in more detail. For striking results, the potential weaknesses can be filtered out by more dimensions. The drill-downs can be done, for instance, timewise to a daily level and ultimately down to a single activity level. For single process instances – in this case finance requests – every process step can be analyzed down to an attribute level. This means that the concrete weak points are identified and improvement activities such as training, system improvements or capacity planning can be derived immediately.

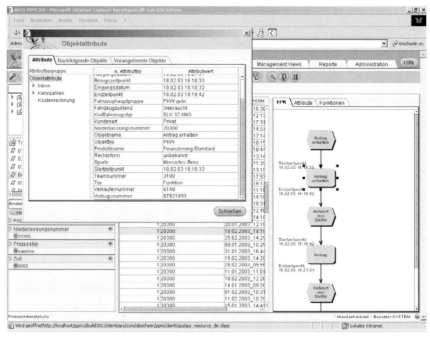

Fig. 12. Non-Automated Decisions per Operational Business Unit Over Time

For those teams which are significantly off-target or show a negative trend, single finance request processes will be analyzed. Striking results in combination of different dimensions can be automatically uncovered with the PPM Process Mining functionality. Process Mining woulde.g. detect all those finance request processes where the actual cycle time for different customer segments, brands or the dimension "external organization" is more than 20% above plan. Furthermore, those periods in which we had the most significant deviations can be analyzed. It might be those deviations occurred mostly during vacation time, during specific times of the day or when the staff was not complete due to absence.

In addition to depicting single-process instances, process instances can be aggregated into one consolidated event-driven process chain (EPC).

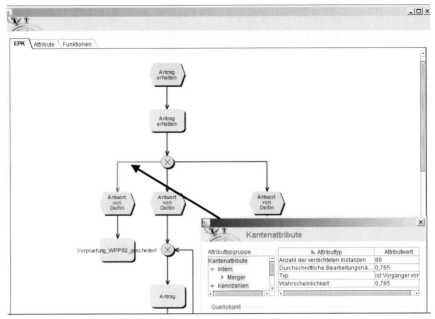

Fig. 13. Aggregated Process Chain for one Team

The probabilities for every single process path are depicted in this EPC. The different aggregated EPCs can be analyzed per dimension. It could be depicted if the process is done differently for cars than for trucks or differently for Mercedes-Benz cars than for Chrysler cars. Most importantly, we have already detected significant differences in succeeding with the initial credit check per team.

5.6 Defining Potentials for Improvement

The analysis sequence across various levels proves that any level can serve as starting point for process improvements:

- Management and Controlling level from an OPI perspective,
- Process Owner level per analyzing trend and from comparisons
- Operations level by looking closely at single process instances.

The Process Owners should be responsible for selecting, prioritizing and applying the identified improvement activities. This is also where the success of these improvement activities should be continuously monitored.

5.7 Communicating Results, Follow-Up

A key benefit for business process management lies in the transparency of improvement activities. The effectiveness of these activities can now be comprehended. Improvements become immediately visible not only in the KPI trends but also in pinpointing the affected business processes.

For example, for the Easyline process, a key contributor to the degree of business process automation is the entered data quality at the point of sale. Incomplete, incorrect or implausible data interrupt the automated business process and ultimately require costly manual interaction. Let's assume, we apply improvements such as a user training campaign and in parallel we implement plausibility checks into the data entering system. By closely monitoring the trend of the OPI, DC Bank will now be able to easily validate the success of these improvements.

The experience gained will enhance future planning, budgeting or auditing cycles as well as future improvement initiatives. Process Performance Management supports the objective of a "Best Practice Approach" if tied into cross-organizational knowledge transfer by benchmarking continuously. Thus the approach becomes a key influencer to the success of DaimlerChrysler Bank.

6   Summary and Outlook

The first phase of the ARIS PPM implementation promised to measure and improve the return on business process automation for the finance request process, called Easyline, supported by Vitrias BusinessWare as EAI layer. Conceptually and technically, all the involved parties at DC Bank from the business side, the controlling and from the technical side were very satisfied and consequently decided to purchase the appropriate ARIS PPM license.

The key operational performance indicator for the success of the Business Process Automation initiative is the "Level of Automation". Without PPM, DC Bank measured the OPI manually and was already able to see that initially, the measure was below expectations even though continuous measuring and transparency of the underlying finance request processes were missing. Now, with ARIS PPM, DC Bank can find out why a finance decision had to be made manually and what needs to be done in the business process to improve the automation of various decisions. Dramatic cost savings, higher customer satisfaction due to fast responses and a stronger relationship to the dealer are the expected results. More process-related details as to why finance proposals failed will be offered. In addition, existing Easyline reporting will be substituted by ARIS PPM, which means a shift from static, manual, paper-based reporting to automated, up-to-date and web-based reporting with role-based views.

All relevant roles will benefit differently from ARIS PPM. The business owner has a better baseline to take business process decisions, which lead to improved performance. The IT architects receive a leverage to prove the value of their EAI system for business process automation. The process controllers and analysts get a better picture of their audited subject. As opposed to discussing historical numbers with their dealer regions, they now jointly view the as-is performance and the underlying business process. They are now empowered to describe how the current business process can be improved by comparing it with their internal best practice. This means a complete paradigm shift in the way process controlling is recognized. The process controller becomes the welcomed change agent.

After the first phase of the ARIS PPM implementation was compelling, DC Bank set the requirements for the second phase. Different process owners already contacted the process controlling group to be considered as early candidate for the ARIS PPM rollout, among them the Customer Call Center and the Leasing Request Process.

Critical success factor was a fully committed head of process controlling who was a firm believer in the need for the paradigm shift and who was able to motivate all the different players in different teams to work together and make this effort a success.

7   References

Hagerty, J.: IDS Scheer elevates Importance of Process Performance Management. AMR Research Inc., Nov. 2002.

Hess, H., Gahse, F.: Geschäftsprozesscontrolling in Handbuch des Controlling, 2001.

Horvath, P.; Mayer, R.: X-Engineering: Neue Potentiale der Prozess Performance erschliessen, in Information Management & Consulting, Oct. 2002.

IDS Scheer AG (Ed.): ARIS Process Performance Manager. White Paper, p. 16-18. Saarbrücken 2002.

Kaplan, R., Norton, D.: The Balanced Scorecard – Measures that drive Performance. Harvard Business Review on Measuring Corporate Performance, p. 123-145. Harvard Business School Press 1998.

Kronz, A., Renner, A., Ramler, K.: Process Performance Measurement in Order Processing; in BWK Das Energie-Fachmagazin; English reprint from no. 11/ 2002, pages 48-51.

Kühl, M.: Geschäftprozesse unter Beobachtung; in Computerwoche No. 10, March 7, 2003.

Loes, G.: Prozessorientierte Einführung und Controlling von CRM-Systemen am Beispiel von Service-Level-Agreements; from A.-W. Scheer, W. Jost (Hrsg.) ARIS in der Praxis: Gestaltung, Implementierung und Optimierung von Geschäftsprozessen, pages 241-265; 2002.

Poirier, P, Ferrara, L., Hayden, F., Neal, D.: The Networked Supply Chain – applying breakthrough business process management technology to meet relentless customer demands; pages 74-84. Boca Raton 2004.

Scheer, A.-W., Abolhassan, F., Jost, W., Kirchmer, M.: Business Process Excellence – ARIS in Practice. Berlin, New York, and others 2002.

EAI Goes Hollywood: Design of a Loosely Coupled Architecture to Manage Critical Business Data Flows at a Major Motion Picture Studio

Colin Western
Major Hollywood Motion Picture Studio

Emmanuel Hadzipetros
IDS Scheer, Inc.

Summary

An often overlooked reality when implementing a major ERP system such as SAP is that the new system will probably never replace all the legacy systems already in place. It generally becomes apparent pretty quickly that the new ERP system will need to share data with the legacy systems. Typically, in the past, these data flows have been managed by writing custom, point-to-point interfaces in which ASCII files are exported from one system and then imported into another for further processing.

Since the late 1990s, Enterprise Application Integration (commonly known as EAI) has captured the imagination of many an IS manager. And no wonder. Its promise is to integrate into a coherent and unified data processing model all applications within an enterprise, including legacy, hand-rolled custom apps and the more powerful breed of ERP systems such as SAP.

When a major Hollywood studio recently undertook a project to produce a Blueprint Design for the implementation of a new SAP system, EAI was high on their list of target accomplishments. There were literally hundreds of legacy systems, many of them hand-rolled on job databases and spreadsheets, that could not be shut down quickly, if ever, and that needed to participate in data flows with SAP. EDI was also a critical consideration. The challenge was to weave all these systems together in a business process-oriented way, including an existing EDI subsystem, into an EAI architecture that leveraged tools and skills that already existed within the organization.

Key Words

SAP, ERP, EAI, ARIS, Enterprise Application Integration, EDI, TrustedLink, Unified Data Model, Unified Data Processing Model, Business Process Design

1   Project Background

1.1 Videos and DVDs: Profits that Keep on Giving

What do Hollywood blockbusters and flops have in common? They all eventually migrate from your neighborhood theater to Video and DVD, providing studios with a long-lasting and steady stream of revenue. This repackaging of entertainment products -- whether movies, mini-series, TV shows, or –concerts -- in video and DVD format for public consumption through retail and rental channels is a multi-billion dollar business that adds handsomely to the bottom line of many a studio.

Recently, a major Hollywood studio decided to replace its aging and highly customized JD Edwards system with SAP to run its Home Video Division. Consultants from IDS-Scheer worked closely with business process owners from the Home Video Division to design an SAP system that would meet the Studio's business processing requirements.

The numbers alone pointed to the complexity of the task: The Home Video business, with more than $1 billion a year in global sales, represents more than 40% of the Studio's annual revenues.

1.2 Managing Complexity

As the enterprise system of record, SAP would be at the heart of the complex data flows required to support this business. It would provide an opportunity to analyze and rationalize business processes and the platform to automate them. In addition, the Home Video implementation was to be the template for a general rollout of SAP throughout the Studio's entire organization.

A key issue that needed to be addressed in considering the implementation of the new ERP system was the integration of SAP with the numerous mission-critical systems that participated in the convoluted data flows that were the lifeblood of the enterprise.

It was a daunting task: SAP needed to integrate effectively with at least 5 major, highly customized systems exchanging data with one another as well as with a myriad of lesser, mostly home-rolled systems that had grown on an as-needed basis over at least 12 years. These lesser systems included everything from one-job Access Databases and Excel spreadsheets to complex mission-critical systems in Finance, vendor-managed inventory and customer replenishment planning.

Integration between these systems was managed entirely through individual point-to-point export and the import of ASCII files.

Furthermore, the data processing that was behind the flow of product from the Studio to consumers was fed almost entirely through massive EDI data exchanges, managed 24x7 in batch schedules, with both customers and vendors.

Again, the numbers speak for themselves. The Home Video Division's billion dollar revenues were generated from about 50 customers, mainly big box stores such as Wal-Mart, Best Buy and Circuit City, in the United States and Canada, all with demanding and highly individual EDI requirements, and literally thousands of ship-to destinations.

The product consumed by these voracious customers was manufactured and packaged offsite by three Vendors, who also managed inventory and provided shipping and delivery services. This Vendor activity was also managed through complex EDI data flows. The new SAP system would keep track of inventory onsite, but inventory would continue to be physically maintained and managed offsite.

1.3 Integrating the Enterprise: Background

The Studio has experimented with Enterprise Application Integration (EAI) in the past and has invested both financial and human resources in Constellar Hub, a centralized interface development and management platform with a hub and spokes architecture that runs on Unix, sits on an Oracle7 database and supports PL SQL processing.

But these efforts had not gone much beyond moving exported ASCII files between directories in different operating systems.

The SAP blueprint provided a golden opportunity to begin serious analysis and design work on an integrated architecture that could eventually be rolled out to the entire enterprise. The philosophy to be followed was that EAI was to be more than an integration platform: It was an approach to systems planning and design that included plans, methods and tools for the consolidation, coordination and integration of applications across and within the enterprise.

1.4 Business Motivation for the Integration Project

The needs and expectations of Home Video's customers are changing. They demand faster response time from the supply chain and some are moving towards web-based AS2 transmission of EDI messages. They want sophisticated value-added services, flexible sales programs and more direct sell-thru and rental sales. And there is also significant downward pressure on pricing.

In short, they want more product, faster and at a cheaper price. The Studio's systems were barely keeping up with current demand and could, at some point, fail, disrupting the business. The Studio clearly needed a more responsive and agile architecture that would improve its ability to respond to its customers' current and future demands.

1.5 Project Scope

The purpose of the project was to provide a blueprint for the implementation of the new SAP system. As a critical part of this effort, the integration sub-project would analyze all data flows impacting on SAP, whether through EDI or internal interfaces, and design an architecture that could accommodate them all in a standard and repeatable way, while leveraging existing skills and architectures.

The project would analyze and identify business processes and system requirements for the new SAP system. Deliverables would include detailed design documents for each of the core processes identified as necessary to running the Home Video business. These included:

- Planning
  - Trend analysis
  - Forecasts
  - Goals and Budgets
- Marketing
- Sales
  - Customer master
  - Revenue share orders
  - Invoice revenue share order
  - Forecast sales
  - Customer rebates and pricing
  - Rental sales performance
  - Sales planning and performance
  - Invoicing
- Procurement
  - Quotes
  - Contracts
  - Purchase orders
  - Purchase requisition
  - Goods receipt processing
  - Invoice receipt processing

- Logistics and distribution
  - Vendor master
  - Material master
  - BOM master
  - Inventory goods movement
  - Perpetual balancing
  - Rework
- Customer Service
  - Sales order entry
  - Pricing and promotions
  - Customer/material determination
  - Returns Credit/Debit notes
  - Delivery and Returns processing
- Financials
  - General Ledger
  - Accounts Payable
  - Accounts Receivable
  - Controlling
  - Profitability Analysis
  - Special Purpose Ledger
- Business Intelligence
  - Business content and info cubes in Finance, Sales and Marketing and Operations.

1.6 Objectives and Goals

1.6.1 Major Business Goals

The new integrated SAP system was expected to lead to common business systems for the global organization that would increase focus on revenue opportunities and support business growth. It would provide a flexible and evolving business environment and enhanced capabilities within sales pricing and order fulfillment processes.

Other expected benefits included:

- Optimized inventory management
- Improved availability of real-time information across all systems

- Support of information access and sharing

- Streamlining processes and reducing waste

- Improved ability to service customers

- Provide an integrated data warehouse with feeds from multiple transactional systems

- Help the Studio to manage future mergers, acquisitions and divestitures more effectively

- Provide faster responses to business initiatives requiring application integration as moving towards XML-based B2B sales and distribution

- Lower or contain costs of producing, selling and distributing product

1.6.2 Major IT Goals

The major IT goal was to design a loosely coupled EAI architecture that would link major legacy systems to SAP, including the existing EDI sub-system, DataMirror's TrustedLink on the AS400, which would be upgraded and extended with an SAP bolt-on to handle mapping and conversion between EDI X12 and SAP's IDOC message formats.

A common platform and set of tools for the development and support of interfaces would sit at the heart of this architecture, lowering or containing critical IT costs.

This platform, built on the Constellar Hub, would manage all data flows between systems and provide a unified metadata repository that would know the data formats used by each participating system, moving the Home Video Division closer to a unified data model. Extraction, cleansing, mapping, posting and moving data between systems would all be handled by the Hub.

The standard architecture would include a central management organization and would support repeatable development methods using a much smaller, and more modern and available, 4GL catalog of programming skills than had been traditional at the Studio.

Interfaces would be built by connecting systems to the Hub and then mapping them to a target or source data model within the Hub and not directly to the partner system. This Hub and Spoke interface architecture, with its own application and database servers, would also be scalable and would grow with increased traffic by upgrading existing boxes or adding new ones.

The EAI architecture would be part of an overall approach to interfaces that includes such standard planning and organizational tools as a standard interface development project plan, common development guidelines and naming conventions, logical and technical specs, interface worksheets, EAI Knowledge Base, and change management and version control.

It was a worthy and ambitious goal that the Studio, with the support of IDS Scheer consultants and the ARIS methodology, set for themselves in this project. It was no less than an attempt to transform the landscape from a largely undocumented mass of individual systems engaged in point-to-point data communications to a unified enterprise data and business processing infrastructure that could quickly and painlessly plug in a new system by putting in a new data connector, created in a common manner, between it and the central Hub.

2   Data Arteries: Building an Integrated Data Architecture to run the Business

2.1 What we are Trying to Change: The Existing Architecture

It's difficult to speak of an existing architecture at the Studio because there really isn't one. Interfaces have been added as users have discovered that data was required from another system to complete a particular process or calculation. The systems themselves were built, largely on an ad-hoc basis, over at least 12 years in response to evolving requirements.

The traditional approach to interface design at the Studio has been described as a "non-architected integration" that was inconsistent, non-reusable and undocumented. It hinged on the knowledge of specific individuals and required skills in a large number of mostly older technologies, including, among others:

- RPG and COBOL/JCL
- FTP and e-mail
- XCOM
- Replication Server
- SQR
- Stored Procedures and Triggers
- Unix scripting
- DataJunction
- ProComm
- OmniConnect / CIS
- BCP / Database Import/Export and ODBC
- DirectConnect / MDI
- Sybase Open Client

There is a simplified view of the interfaces between and within the major systems in the Home Video Division in figure 1 below.

Bear in mind that the web of individually connected systems illustrated below represents one business unit, albeit the largest single producer of revenue in the enterprise. This network of data arteries was, in turn, connected through its individual parts to other systems at an enterprise level, using the same kind of point-to-point interfaces illustrated below.

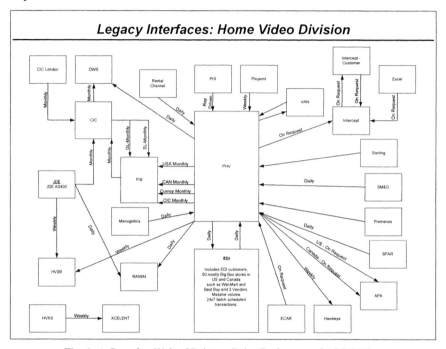

Fig. 1. A Complex Web of Point-to-Point Exchanges of ASCII Files

2.2 The Vision: Integrated Data Flows to Support Automated Business Processes

All systems that feed into SAP directly or indirectly, including the TrustedLink EDI sub-system, major business systems such as Production and Customer Replenishment Planning and Corporate Financials, as well as the myriad of one-job hand-rolled databases and spreadsheets, would flow through the common EAI Hub.

A cleaner design overall, although each individual interface would pass through more steps than in the old world.

The process for an inbound (into SAP; outbound would follow the same process flow in reverse) interface would connect the source and target systems through extraction into a Transformation Server (Publisher) in the source system's environment into a Transformation Server (Subscriber) within the Constellar Hub's Unix environment.

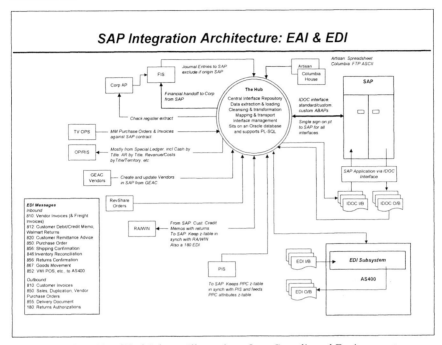

Fig. 2. A Simplified Schema Illustrating a Less Complicated Environment

In most cases, the Hub would log into the source system and kick off the extract processing. The same would be true for the target system, including SAP.

From the Publisher, the file would pass into the Hub repository built on an Oracle7 database and undergo mapping and conversion, from the external to the SAP expected format, by the Hub's mapping engine. The result would be an ASCII file (custom- or IDOC-formatted) that would then be passed into an in-directory in the SAP NT environment and picked up by a custom or standard SAP program for inbound processing and posting.

File movements between systems would be handled by FTP jobs kicked off by the Hub's scheduling utility. SAP programs for inbound processing would be called directly by the Hub.

Control reports within the Hub would report on success or failure in either direction for every record passed.

There are more processing steps involved per individual interface than in the old world, but the process (and the tools used to implement it) just described remains the same for all interfaces, regardless of source and target system, resulting in fewer moving, disjoined pieces across the entire landscape.

This process is illustrated in figure 3 below, which provides an overview of major inbound supply-chain systems processing, including EDI.

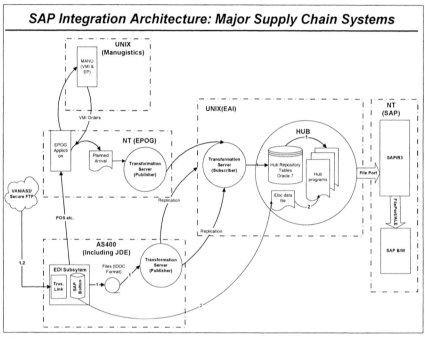

Fig. 3. A Little More Detail Illustrating the Various Steps Required for Each Connection

The EDI process is particularly important, considering how much critical data will pass into SAP via EDI. The EDI processing chain is illustrated in figure 4.

SAP treats EDI as an interface between SAP and an EDI sub-system using IDOC (Intermediate Document) messages to move extracted SAP out or partner data in for posting to SAP transactions.

Typically, mapping and conversion chores between SAP IDOCs and EDI messages are handled in the EDI sub-system. This will be true in the new environment as well. But the Studio has settled on a single architecture for all interfaces and EDI is being treated in the same way. In some cases, also, there is additional processing required to support EDI that will be handled in the EDI sub-system.

EDI processing follows two paths into and out of SAP, depending on whether or not additional processing is required for the document being transmitted.

One involves direct transmission into (or out of) SAP from the EDI sub-system through the Hub. The Hub still controls the traffic but the EDI sub-system handles mapping and conversions duties.

The second follows the same path that other interfaces will follow. The EDI sub-system will continue to handle mapping and conversion, but the IDOC moves into the Transformation Server for further processing in the Hub before being sent to an in-directory in the SAP environment, where standard inbound IDOC processing is kicked off by the Hub.

This process is illustrated in figure 4 below.

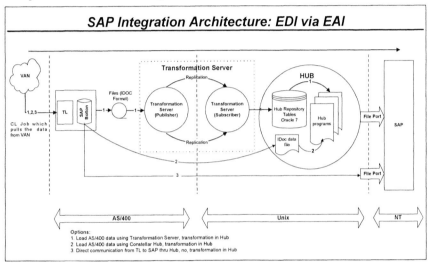

Fig. 4. EAI and the Inbound EDI Processing Chain

2.3 A First Step: Looking to the Future

The basis for the development of the EAI architecture was the ARIS framework, which structures the various views on a business process: organization, functions, data, deliverables, control. The key for this initiative was the data view on the processes.

Defining this architecture begins with understanding the data requirements of SAP and the other key enterprise systems that will remain. The Hub provides the focal point for data integration, for a unified data model that other systems will plug into it as they are brought online.

There will be a consistent and rational data model that encompasses all of the enterprise's key business systems to serve as the foundation for business process rationalization and integration. For the first time, the Studio will begin to really know its data. This knowledge will bring increased flexibility and responsiveness, better control of the supply chain and improved ability to adopt new processes.

One scenario for an integrated enterprise is illustrated in figure 5 below. It puts the Hub at the heart of the enterprise, with its central data repository describing critical corporate data that must be used across systems, the key to maintaining usable data flows between different applications across the enterprise, effectively transforming all participating applications into a cooperative business processing platform.

But the architecture illustrated below still essentially provides a batch-processing regime. All data movements, all export or import jobs into and out of each system need to be scheduled using an enterprise scheduling tool, in this case Maestro.

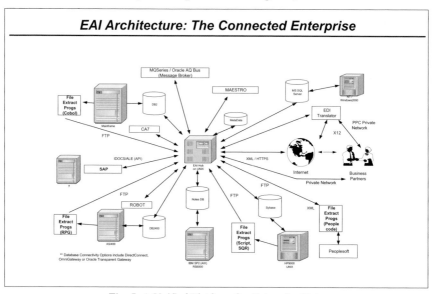

Fig. 5. A Unified Platform for Enterprise Data

It is a huge step, but still not the final goal. Success of the SAP implementation and the new EAI architecture is a major milestone along a long and winding road. Near real-time information flow and greatly reduced supply-chain cycles, even same-day shipment of product, are ultimate goals.

XML messaging wrapped up in SOAP envelopes requesting and providing data via HTTP from Web Services discovered in UDDI directories offers great promise for the future, assuming that emerging standards are codified and widely adopted, knowledge spreads and resources are put into hard (equipment) and soft (people and skills) infrastructure.

The Studio is actively studying the potential of this exciting technology with the hope that the new architecture being defined (Constellar Hub supports XML mapping) will be the foundation for the evolution of the intelligent interfaces of the future, both within the enterprise and in its relationships with its partners.

3   Project Approach: Integrating People for Success

3.1 Project Timelines and Deliverables

The Business Blueprint Project ran for three months. Its prime purpose was to define the Studio's business practices and parameters, to understand business goals and structures, and to determine how SAP can be configured and customized to accommodate these.

The goal was to provide a system design, a Blueprint, to support the future state of the Studio's business as defined by the mapping of SAP processes envisioned by the project team.

This included identifying the gaps between standard SAP and the Studio's to-be processes, identifying and quantifying the development effort required to customize the new environment (whether in SAP or external systems).

In addition, the underlying technical requirements to support the business design needed to be worked out.

The major deliverables of the Blueprint Phase were:

• Definition of a Project Charter detailing project objectives, scope, planning, methodology, issue management, monitoring and standards and procedures

• Technical Design, encompassing physical infrastructure requirements, including sizing of servers, and definition of Basis requirements and installation of a preliminary sandbox for development work

• Blueprint Documents detailing the design for every technical and business process identified as in scope (see Project Scope above)

• A RICE List identifying all Reports, Interfaces, Conversions, Enhancements and SAPScript forms that needed to be built to support the business

• Blueprint Document outlining conversion and interface strategy, including design of an EAI architecture to tie together EDI, SAP and all interfaces identified as required for SAP

• Project Plans detailing tasks required to complete the Blueprinted system

- Training Plans

- Project Organizational Structure

- Change Management Assessment

3.2 Organizing and Integrating the Effort

IDS Scheer provided the SAP consultants, both functional and technical, and the methodology, based on the ARIS framework, to the project team. From the Studio came business process owners, legacy analysts and programmers, integration specialists, EDI developers and assorted consultants with specialized technical knowledge of existing processes and systems.

Day-to-day leadership of the team was in the hands of a joint project management team, composed of an IDS Scheer and two Studio project managers: one from MIS and the other from the Business. The project management team reported to a Steering Committee composed of mid-management decision-makers, which in turn reported to an Executive Steering Committee that included the CEO, CIO and other high-ranking management from the Business. The Executive Steering Committee had ultimate responsibility for project direction and sign-offs.

The project team was divided into 6 core sub teams focused on business processes, including:

- Finance and Controlling

- Sales and Distribution

- Purchasing and Inventory Management

- Business Warehouse

- Organizational Change Management

- Technical Infrastructure

Each team had a core membership composed of a process leader from the Studio, supported by a Studio MIS team member and an IDS Scheer consultant and an extended team of additional resources that included international employees.

The bulk of the work of identifying and mapping in scope business processes to SAP was done in intensive, 5-hour workshops that ran on a two-week rolling basis over most of the life of the project. Workshop topics were changed only when the previous topic had been exhausted.

There were also workshops that examined points of integration between processes bringing together a number of teams at the same time.

The Technical Infrastructure team coordinated the efforts of 5 sub-teams that worked on key technical issues including:

- Basis Infrastructure

- Authorizations

- ABAP Development

- Application Integration (EDI, EAI and Data Conversion)

- Software Change Management

3.3 The Process of Discovery

We are primarily concerned here with the work of the Technical Infrastructure team, particularly the ABAP and Application Integration sub-teams. These two teams, led by an IDS Scheer ABAP consultant with extensive experience in data conversion and integration of SAP with external systems, were directly responsible for the design of the EAI architecture, including the EDI interfaces that emerged from the Blueprint Phase.

The work of these teams was largely dependent on the progress made by the functional teams in a number of areas, including:

- Design of business processing cycles dependent on EDI, for example, the entire Sales Orders processing cycle including the initial order, returns processing, shipping and delivery, invoicing and payment

- Design of business processing cycles dependent on the flow of data between SAP and external Home Video systems, such as journal entries in SAP from the Corporate Financial System

- Identification of gaps between standard SAP business transactions and the processing steps required to complete Home Video's business processes

- Identification of new requirements to handle business processes not available in standard SAP, whether through a custom-written program or by tweaking the code behind an IDOC in a customer exit

These variables determined the pace and direction for the work of identifying programming requirements for SAP (and sometimes external systems) and of designing an integrated architectural approach to EDI and EAI.

Requirements needed to be collected, and this was largely accomplished by reading through the documentation produced by the functional business process teams and extensive interviews with the relevant functional consultants, business process owners, legacy analysts and programmers, EDI developers, Home Video consultants and outside experts including vendors responsible for the various systems that needed to be integrated.

As business requirements firmed up and identification of development objects proceeded, the existing EDI architecture was examined in detail with the help of the EDI and in-house integration teams. Every transmission was plotted and analyzed and mapped against corresponding data containers (IDOCs, BAPIs) in SAP. Gaps were identified and solutions researched in SAP, usually involving extension of IDOCs and custom code in user exits.

The process was the same for the interfaces between SAP and legacy systems. They had to be identified and plotted and technical gaps defined. From this, a list of programming requirements began to grow.

At the same time, architecture was being examined. The Studio already owned Constellar Hub, but was also considering Mercator for both EAI and EDI. Research was done on EDI sub-systems, since this was the critical piece. Vendors were consulted. A decision was made to keep TrustedLink on the AS400 to leverage existing skills within the organization. But it would need to be upgraded and an SAP bolt-on installed to read in the structure of SAP IDOCs for mapping to X12 messages.

The issue became how best to integrate the existing EDI sub-system, all of the other interfaces and SAP into a coherent data-processing model without breaking the bank or taking unnecessary risks with exotic and untried technology. The Constellar Hub had been used by the Studio in a pilot project, and its general operating principles were known. Its Oracle database and support for PL SQL was considered a big plus. The Hub was therefore the obvious starting point.

The EAI architecture emerged thereafter through the cooperative effort of a large group of people supported every step of the way by team leaders and project management. The initial architectural design was produced by IDS Scheer as the larger SAP design effort proceeded.

This design was continuously updated with input from the various business process teams as they finalized their system designs, as well as from different groups within the Studio's IS Department and among business process owners. Through a continual cycle of meetings, brainstorming sessions, informal conversations with users, developers and vendors, research, writing and drawing, a final Blueprint document emerged describing a strategy and detailing an architecture for rationalizing and managing enterprise interfaces.

This Blueprint design document was signed off on and became the starting point for building the EAI architecture in the Realization phase.

4   Results

4.1 Achievements

The SAP system design that emerged from the workshops led by IDS Scheer was signed off by the Executive Steering Committee. Through the hard work and co-operative efforts of all involved, the Blueprint successfully defined the best SAP system that could be built considering the business requirements, time constraints, future plans and available resources of the Studio. Every consulting firm that was invited to bid on the Final Realization Phase of the SAP implementation project, had to bid on the Blueprint that IDS Scheer developed in cooperation with the Studio's employees.

The cooperative approach adopted by IDS Scheer and its client partners proved to be a winning combination. Despite fierce competition from larger consulting companies with more resources, IDS Scheer, with its impressive combination of talent, methodology, technical vision, deep SAP implementation experience and knowledge of the client's business, won the final contract

4.1.1 Defining a Vision for the Future

Defining the EAI architecture was all about defining a vision of how disparate data sources and applications could be harnessed to better serve the future of the enterprise. It pointed to the potential of a unified data model providing a platform for ongoing rationalization and automation of business process. An additional bonus: The cooperative effort involved in producing the work provided an effective model for future projects.

4.1.2 Bringing People Together

Application integration is also about bringing people together into a cooperative enterprise aimed at improving everybody's working life. The EAI architectural design that came out of Blueprint was a joint effort between IDS Scheer and a number of different groups and organizations within the Home Video Division's IS Department, including Applications, EDI, EAI and Infrastructure, as well as a large number of business owners.

Bringing all these people together in a common effort, in an environment as busy and dynamic as the Studio's, was an impressive and effective achievement.

4.2 Consistency With Defined Goals

4.2.1 All Major Objectives Being Met

All major achievements outlined in sections 1.5 and 1.6 were met. A design document was produced that formed the basis for the subsequent Realization phase and that is still driving the basic design of the EAI architecture. This architecture is being built and tested, and there is every expectation that it will be implemented successfully at the end of the Realization phase (scheduled for spring 2004).

In addition to the concrete achievement of designing a system that is being built, and simplifying and rationalizing enterprise data flows, the Studio is well on its way to having a unified data model.

5   Lessons Learned

5.1 Analyze Until it Hurts

All systems need to be analyzed, including legacy systems that may have little or no documentation but are locked up in the heads of one or two consultants. It's worth the effort to dig out this information and document it.

5.2 Need for Enterprise Scheduler Highlighted

The complexity of all the moving parts in the EAI architecture is daunting. The design effort underlined the need for a central management tool that would be used to schedule and monitor all these moving parts. In addition, error reporting, controls and balancing all need to be considered.

5.3 Communicate, Communicate

People and organizations need to work effectively together. In order for this to happen, communications are absolutely critical. Good communications are the glue for cooperation. Communications need to flow in all directions, not just from the top down or the bottom up. Everybody needs to be on the same page.

A Process-Oriented Approach to Implementation of Microsoft Axapta at Bowne Global Solutions

Rajiv Lajmi
IDS Scheer SME Midatlantic

Jeff Michaels
IDS Scheer SME Midatlantic

Chris Snyder
IDS Scheer SME Midatlantic

Summary

When implementing a standard ERP package in a global environment, oftentimes the choice between customization and process change can be difficult to make. In order to design and configure a system that will satisfy all stakeholders in many countries conducting the same business, and minimize implementation costs, standardized global processes must be formulated.

The overall goal of a joint initiative between IDS-Scheer and Bowne Global Solutions was to define global accounting processes across more than 20 countries, and configure Microsoft Axapta accordingly to support those processes. The specific business goals were to reduce financial closing time to 5 days, significantly lower total cost of ownership, and to centralize finance and accounting functions.

Key Words

ARIS, Axapta, Reference Model, Business Process Definition, eEPC, Conference Room Pilot, Business Process, Configuration Map, Test Script

1   Customer Background

Bowne Global Solutions (BGS) is a leading provider of translation, localization, technical writing and interpretation services to enable businesses to deliver locally relevant and culturally connected products, services and communications anywhere in the world.

Headquartered in New York City, Bowne Global Solutions was created in 1997 through the acquisition of four leading localization services providers – IDOC, GECAP, Pacifitech, ME&TA and I&G Com. Mendez, a leading provider of globalization solutions in Europe, was acquired in 2001, followed by Berlitz Global-NET in 2002. BGS operates in 24 countries across the world.

2   As-Is Situation

As a result of the numerous mergers and acquisitions, BGS was left with several different enterprise systems to operate with as a consolidated organization. PeopleSoft was the most widely used system across the organization, both within the US and worldwide. Other locations ran a variety of systems including Epicor, Sage as well as earlier versions of PeopleSoft. To meet local accounting, reporting, and invoicing requirements, some countries ran a local solution, and would then send financial statements to the corporate headquarters for reporting in PeopleSoft.

Financial consolidations were a manual process completed by importing monthly trial balances into PeopleSoft's general ledger for countries not running PeopleSoft. When all of the countries' data was imported into PeopleSoft and verified, it was then exported to Hyperion for inclusion in the financial statements of BGS' parent company, Bowne. As a result, BGS was faced with a lengthy 20-30 day monthly closing process. In addition, the utilization of disparate ERP solutions left BGS with dissimilar business processes across the organization, leading to great inefficiencies.

As part of the overall corporate IT strategy, Microsoft Business Solutions, Axapta was selected as the ERP system to replace PeopleSoft and other systems used by BGS' international subsidiaries. In addition, BGS decided to rollout globally their homegrown job cost system, Gemini, which was integrated only with PeopleSoft and Epicor. Gemini tracks localization and translation project information such as purchase orders, timesheet tracking, customer invoicing, and project milestone tracking and revenue recognition. Countries not utilizing PeopleSoft and Epicor updated projects in Gemini manually. Gemini is now integrated with Axapta using Microsoft BizTalk Server.

3 Motivation to Use a Business Process Automation Solution

The decision to replace BGS' ERP systems with Axapta was primarily based on the following factors:

1. The unacceptable 20 days that it took BGS, a unit of a publicly traded company, to close the books each month.

2. The lack of centralized control of, and visibility into, financial information of country operations.

3. The high cost of supporting the various systems that BGS utilized.

4. The need to maintain two systems in some countries in order to meet corporate and local regulatory requirements.

4 Why Axapta?

Axapta is a fully functional ERM system provided by Microsoft Business Solutions. Its capabilities include Finance, Trade and Logistics, Manufacturing, Distribution, Human Resources, Project Accounting and Customer Relationship Management.

The specific Axapta functionality that was critical to BGS includes multi-language, multi-currency, intercompany transactions, and import and export via XML. Multiple companies, currencies, and languages can all be deployed in one database.

The Axapta Solution can be deployed in either a 2-tier or 3-tier (fat or thin client) environment or a combination of both.

5 Project Goals

5.1 Standardizing Global Business Processes With ARIS

The need to persistently focus on internal business processes becomes the decisive competitive factor for companies. In this context, clearly and uniformly defined responsibilities, maximum transparency of structures, a homogenous communication basis integrating all company levels, and streamlined project management based on corporate vision and strategy, are vital for success. But only a holistic view of business processes would enable a company to recognize, streamline and support interconnected processes through optimized information- system environments.

A holistic view of business processes is what BGS desired at the start of the Axapta implementation. Since BGS operates in 24 countries across the world, it became imperative that a common means of communicating business processes across the organization be conceived.

As a result, the development of "To-Be" business processes, incorporating Axapta into the process mix (BGS' stated mandate for the project was 90% adherence to "out-of-the-box" Axapta functionality as the basis for "To-Be" processes) became a key objective of the discovery and analysis phases of the implementation project. The first step in the process-mapping exercise was the definition of key project objectives to be satisfied for the implementation to be considered a success. These objectives, in turn, had to incorporate BGS' organizational goals and strategic business vision. The following diagram was used as a constant reminder during the process definition phase of the exercise.

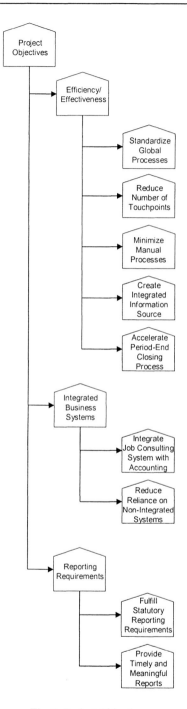

Fig. 1. Project Objectives

5.2 Business Goals

- To reduce global periodic financial close time from 25 days to 5 days.
- Centralized financial reporting by country and business unit.
- Integration of financial system (Axapta) to operational system (Gemini) across all countries.
- To significantly reduce total cost of ownership.

5.3 IT-Related Goals

- Global Infrastructure with global control (one database, one data center).
- Upward as well as downward scalability.
- Limit customization, use 90% standard functionality.

6   Project Scope

IDS Scheer SME agreed to implement Axapta for BGS in 24 countries in a time-frame of approximately ten months in total. The scope of the implementation project included the automation and implementation of the following business processes:

- General Ledger
- Electronic Banking
- Fixed Assets
- Financial Reporting and Consolidations
- Accounts Payable
- Accounts Receivable
- Purchase Orders
- Sales Orders
- Integrations
- Integration to BGS' homegrown project management system "Gemini"

7   Implementation Approach

7.1 Business Process Definition

In line with the project objectives identified, the process definition phase began with the use of an Axpata reference model as the starting point. Developed by IDS Scheer SME, the reference model provided BGS with a process framework that would help key project participants understand the business processes, objects, and variables involved in using Axapta. As a result, the reference model would become a mechanism to train key project participants, communicate the implementation approach across the organization, and ensure the integrity of the "To-Be" business process.

As a first step, an evaluation of the baseline processes was performed to determine how to leverage Axapta's pre-defined business processes, and take advantage of the full scope of the software's functionality. Key operational areas that had the most impact on competitive performance were then included in process discussions in order to decide on the "to-be" environment. Best practices from Axapta's standard functionality were also incorporated into the "to-be" processes.

This exercise focused on identifying the various tasks performed, departments and positions involved, systems used, and documents involved while performing those tasks, with a specific focus on operations and finance. Throughout the exercise, core project team participants were pushed to view their business entities and employees' activities in a structured, flow-like manner.

The processes at BGS were documented using the "Extended Event-Driven Process Chain" (eEPC) method within ARIS. By means of an eEPC, the procedure of a business process is described as a logical chain of events. Since events trigger functions and can be the outcome of functions, core team members were made to realize the inputs, outputs, and impact of each path in an eEPC. Participants were forced to structure their thinking around business processes, and clearly define the outcomes of process splits and dependencies.

The end-result of the BGS "to-be" processes are described at four levels:

Level 1: This level is composed of the core BGS process of pre-sales, pre-production, production, and post-production functions. This model is represented using a Value-Added Chain. In addition, support processes that touch all of the core functions are also represented at the highest level.

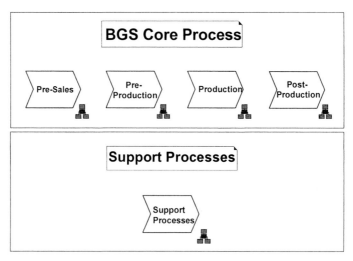

Fig. 2. Level 1 Processes

Level 2: In Level 2, each function in level 1 is decomposed into sub-major processes, also Value-Added Chains. For BGS, the Level 2 functions delve into their major lines of business, viz. localization and translation, interpretation, and technical writing services.

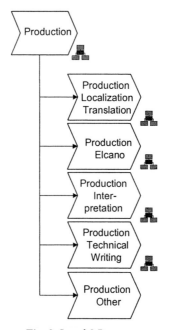

Fig. 3. Level 2 Processes

Level 3: Each Level 2 function is decomposed into an eEPC at Level 3. At this third level, the relationships between positions, functions and the systems involved are also represented. Given that BGS was going to implement Axapta, this representation was critical in order to identify any potential integration points.

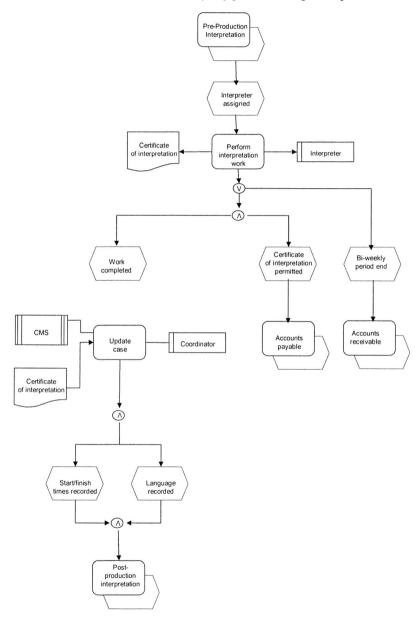

Fig. 4. Level 3 Processes

Level 4: All Level 3 functions relating to Axapta are decomposed into an eEPC at Level 4. At this fourth level, the user's interaction with the system has been represented. This includes some specific fields and Axapta functions that need to be executed in order for transactions to be posted.

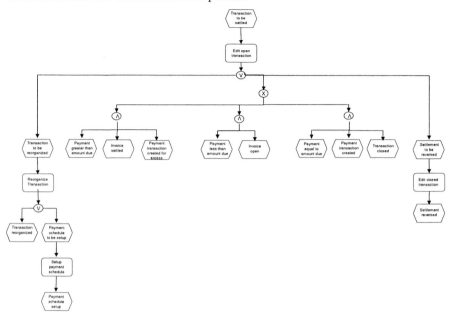

Fig. 5. Level 4 Processes

One of the many challenges faced during the process documentation process was to incorporate functionality provided by BGS' many homegrown IT systems along with that provided by Axapta. As such, it was integral to identify any and all integration points between these systems and Axapta. A Program Chart diagram was used to represent all identified system interfaces in a structured manner. This allowed technical teams on both sides, IDS' and BGS', to prioritize, document, and execute these process interfaces.

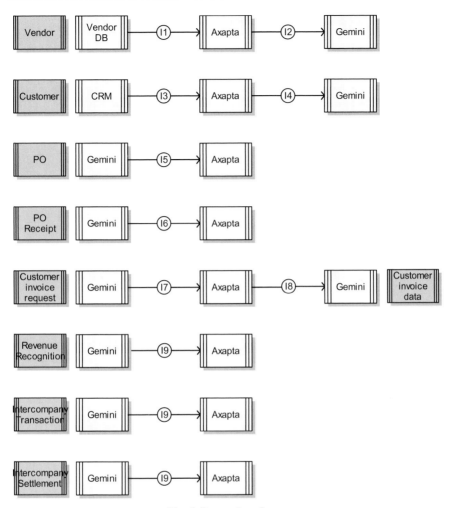

Fig. 6. System Interfaces

7.1 BGS Axapta IT Architecture

The following diagram displays the Axapta IT architecture at BGS after implementing Axapta and several integrations with Gemini.

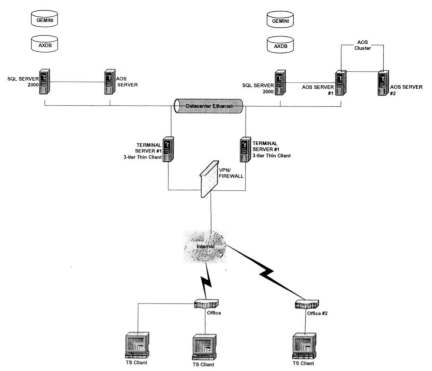

Fig. 7. Overall Network Topography

7.2 Configuration

Based on deliverables from the business process definition phase, a comprehensive business requirements document was prepared that formed the basis for all system setup and configuration. As part of this process, the configuration map was then completed for each country based on local requirements. The configuration map is a replica of the setup and configuration options for the various modules in Axapta, and reflects these options for the particular installation. These serve as documentation for system setup and as a baseline for subsequent changes to the system. A sample configuration map is provided below.

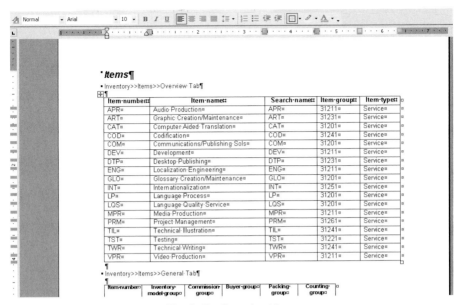

Fig. 8. Configuration Map

As the configuration was being finalized, these configuration maps were updated for each module implemented.

7.3 Conference Room Pilot

Upon completion of the base configuration, super-user training was conducted in order to gain participation and input from key participants. One milestone requirement of the project was the successful completion of the conference room pilot, for which the core project team and super-users were invited. To facilitate this pilot, participants were issued test scripts and asked to provide feedback on the configuration after they had run through the scripts. Such feedback served as a useful guide to modify any setup within the system, as well as a form of documentation that the setup had been tested and confirmed by the client. Given that modifications were necessary based on requirements, four testing cycles were planned and executed. A sample test script is provided below.

7.4 Go-Live Strategy

Since 24 countries were involved in the implementation, IDS Scheer SME recommended a phased approach to going live on Axapta. According to the recommendation, all 24 countries would go live in a 5-month timeframe. Ireland was selected as a pilot site to go live in mid-October 2003. A pilot site was selected so as to resolve any potential issues before any other sites went live. Eight sites then went live in mid-November, followed by two sites in December, ten sites in January 2004, and three sites in February.

8   Results

8.1 Measuring Against Project Goals

Before the selection of Axapta as the ERP solution of choice, BGS laid out specific project goals that needed to be achieved in order for the project to be considered a success. These goals can be divided primarily into two categories, Business goals and IT goals.

8.2 Five-Day Period-End Close

The first business goal was to reduce the amount of time needed to close each accounting period. BGS targeted a 20-day reduction in the time it took to close the accounting period in each country as a specific target. Ireland, the pilot site, was able to close the month of November, 2003, on the fifth business day of the following month, thus enabling us to state preliminarily that this major objective was achieved. It is expected that as the other countries come online, they will also recognize similar reductions in period closing times.

8.3 Centralized Reporting by Country and Business Unit

The software tool used to facilitate the shorting of the closing cycle goal was Microsoft's FRx financial reporting solution. BGS and IDS Scheer participated in the beta program for FRx for Axapta; previously, FRx was not available for Axapta. In the testing phase, of the project, BGS and IDS Scheer were able to successfully run reports through FRx that illustrated both individual and consolidated results for the first eight countries that went live, as well as reports that broke down individual and consolidated results by business unit. We can confidently say that the goal of centralized reporting by country and business unit is being met.

8.4 Integration of Financial System (Axapta) to Operational System (Gemini) Across all Countries

The completion of integration between Axapta and Gemini was a collaborative effort between resources from both BGS and IDS Scheer. Developers from IDS Scheer trained in Axapta's X++ programming language worked hand-in-hand with in-house developers from BGS' California R&D center. The end results of the integration work were:

- Purchase order and receipt transactions originating in Gemini and flowing through to Axapta; in addition, invoice data from Axapta was sent back to Gemini.

- Customer invoices originating in Gemini and flowing through to Axapta, and then being printed in Axapta.

Throughout the CRP and the Pilot Go Live in Ireland, the integration functioned as designed.

8.5 Global Infrastructure With Global Control

Excepting the Gemini Application and failover database servers in Dublin, Ireland, all of the servers utilized in BGS' deployment of Axapta reside in their corporate offices in Piscataway, NJ. Users connect via pure thin client or Terminal Service. With this architecture, BGS was able to meet its above-stated goal of global infrastructure and global control.

Administration, maintenance, and future version upgrades can all be rolled out from the Piscataway data center. Corporate Accounting and Finance users can perform inquiries, post transactions, and run reports on any of the countries that their role requires them to have access to – in their native language.

8.6 Upward as Well as Downward Scalability

Across BGS, the need for an integrated ERP solution varies widely from the corporate offices, where 12 plus users manage the Accounting and Finance function of the entire organizations to subsidiaries such as Chile and Brazil, where only 1 or 2 users utilize the system primarily for accounting.

Nonetheless, BGS and IDS-Scheer were able to utilize an identical roll-out plan to all countries regardless of size; moreover, the thin client capabilities of Axapta enabled BGS to implement cost-effectively without making large infrastructure investments in countries where only a small number of users were present.

8.7 Limited Customization of Axapta

Early on in the project, BGS and IDS-Scheer agreed to significantly limit the amount customization to the Axapta system. Wherever possible, it was decided that BGS would undergo a process change in order to adhere to Axapta's best practices. In certain situations, however, this was not possible owing to legal and business requirements. Any resulting customizations were then built utilizing development tools such as X++ and VB.NET. Overall system configuration was defined using the setup, field, and logic options, as well as report writing that would not affect the inherent Axapta code base.

This goal was achieved largely due to the use of the Axapta reference model as a guide to establishing global processes and workflow, as well as limiting customization to three major areas of "must have" functionality not inherent in Axapta:

- Integration to Gemini

- EFT formats for payments

- Local statutory financial reporting

9   Lessons Learned

9.1 Language and Localization Add Another Level of Complexity to ERP Rollouts

Rolling out an ERP solution over 24 countries was an extremely complex undertaking. We were able to successfully complete this project because of the Business Process Mapping exercise and the execution of a Conference Room Pilot.

The Business Process Mapping exercise, using the ARIS Toolkit, identified where the common processes ended and where the local processes and requirements began. We were then able to translate those processes and requirements into country-specific functionality through the localization inherent to Axapta as well as configuration and a relatively minor amount of customization.

The Conference Room Pilot was the vehicle that enabled users to validate the local functionality configured. The local users' input was invaluable given that they are the ones who work day in and day out in these countries and are an excellent source of knowledge regarding local requirements. There were some revisions to the configuration based on feed back from the CRP, but the up-front Business Process Mapping exercise greatly minimized it.

U.S. Army Logistics Process Automation Based on SAP NetWeaver Technology

Thomas R. Gulledge
George Mason University

Greg Huntington
Enterprise Integration, Inc.

Wael Hafez
IDS Scheer, Inc.

Georg Simon
IDS Scheer, Inc.

Summary

The Army logistics system is a complex series of processes, organizations, doctrines, procedures and automated systems. Historically, the system has been separated into two management levels: wholesale, which typically includes Army Materiel Command (AMC), Defense Logistics Agency (DLA), and the industrial base; and retail, which includes all customer organizations at theater and below. Doctrinally, however, the system is segregated into three levels: strategic, operational, and tactical. In recent years, decisions have been made to enable these domains using commercial standard software whenever appropriate. This paper describes an architectural planning approach for designing a standard software solution that combines the two management levels of Army logistics.

Key Words

Logistics, Enterprise Architecture, Standard Software, ERP, SAP, Public Sector, NetWeaver, Master Data Management

1   Project Background

The Army enterprise vision is "A fully integrated environment that builds, sustains, and generates war-fighting capability through a fully integrated logistics enterprise based upon collaborative planning, knowledge management, and best-business practices." To bring the vision to fruition, the Army is exploiting new Information Technology (IT) through the Logistics Modernization Program (LMP) and the Global Combat Support System - Army (G-Army) programs. The Army has selected the SAP standard software solution to enable these modernization efforts. Through business process reengineering (BPR) and by adopting the best business practices embedded in the SAP software, the Army intends to develop the Army Logistics Enterprise (ALE). These modernization efforts focus on an integrated and seamless information system end-state. Currently, there is a plethora of other systems that support Army logistics operations. Action is being taken to integrate, consolidate and delete the old and stovepiped systems as the Army transitions to the SAP standard software solution. The opportunity for the Army to define a fully automated end-to-end logistics enterprise is greatly enhanced through its option for the SAP solution.

The Army fielded its first SAP deployment in July of 2003. The eventual full operational capability (FOC), which occurs in December 2003, will modernize the current two major logistics sustainment IT systems (e.g. Commodity Command Standard System and Standard Depot System). G-Army (SAP) is scheduled for deployment starting in FY2005 with FOC in FY2007. The Army is committed to a sound strategy based on architectural planning which will frame the scope and establish a baseline for follow-on extended enterprise implementations.

To support the transition to a fully integrated solution, the Army was seeking an enterprise architecture that provided for an integrated logistics value chain. The Army's goal was to employ logistics operations knowledge and SAP systems knowledge to develop creative solutions to leverage SAP technology to provide the utmost operationally effective solution to enable the logistics vision.

Hence, the Army made a contract with Enterprise Integration, Inc. (EII) and IDS Scheer, Inc. (IDS) to provide a review and analysis of ongoing activities associated with current logistics programs, along with specific programs and plans that may be expanded to contribute to the desired solution. EII and IDS were asked to develop a solution architecture that supports a web-based SAP solution strategy, taking all Army logistics business processes into account, to include disconnected operations and taskforce reorganization. The scope includes the functions of supply, maintenance, packaging and handling of material, and associated logistics financial functions, ensuring engineering product data is managed and utilized, warehouse functions, industrial base, connectivity to automatic identification technology, and combat support systems such as medical, transportation, personnel, finance, and legal. The enterprise architecture was required to span all major commands (MACOMs) and all echelons in the Army (to include fixed-base and deployed operations). The solution architecture was designed to provide commanders at all levels with ultimate capabilities to build combat power and manage readiness. The Army Logistics Enterprise architecture was also required to align with the Office of the Secretary of Defense (OSD) Future Logistics Enterprise (FLE) architecture and the OSD (Comptroller) Business Enterprise Architecture (BEA).

2   Project Goals

The Army Logistics Enterprise (ALE) architecture was developed by IDS, EII, SAP, and the Gartner Group (Henceforth known as "the Team"). The Team reviewed the Army's business process requirements relative to the business processes supported by the SAP standard software solution. The architecture leveraged the documentation provided from the LMP SAP implementation as well as other relevant documentation. The architecture identified integration opportunities within SAP, as well as interoperability opportunities among operational, tactical, and sustainment business processes to create a fully integrated Army logistics solution. The architecture documents the resulting business processes in accordance with the DoD Architectural Framework (C4ISR). The ALE architecture, as accepted by the US Army, documents the to-be SAP solution for Army logistics.

2.1 Architecture Analysis

This study reviewed the accomplishments of modernization efforts currently underway. This included an analysis of existing operational, technical, systems, and data architectures to determine the SAP software scope, hardware requirements, and communications infrastructure required to meet logistics strategy. The analysis included the rationale for determining the preferred solution, the benefits, and any trade-off analyses. The analysis also included consideration and incorporation of any requirements for the protection of logistics and financial data. The pros and cons of each selected alternative were addressed to include the cost implications and risk associated with each. Data management, data administration, and data synchronization processes and efficiencies were addressed as a part of this analysis. Software, hardware, and configuration control efficiencies and limitations were taken into consideration. The resulting architecture provides a System Interface Description in accordance with the DoD Architecture Framework, which identifies external systems and system component interfaces.

2.2 Integrated Schedule

The team also developed a high-level integrated implementation schedule for realizing the end-to-end logistics vision. The schedule includes the development, transition, and implementation of the proposed solution. This schedule also considered the current SAP fielding schedules and included a recommended fielding plan for all of Army logistics. The integrated schedule analysis addressed those key subsequent steps that the Army needs to take in order to achieve an integrated single enterprise solution. The schedule included training recommendations (to include replacement, refresher training, and institutional training), system updates, technology refresh, and system lifecycle considerations. The schedule addressed opportunities and potential constraints of logistics modernization with an emphasis on the optimization of current modernization schedules along with other emerging Army and Department of Defense (DoD) initiatives.

2.3 Institutionalization of the Enterprise Architecture (EA)

The architecture study encompasses a detailed methodology describing, "How the EA should be used by the Army." The detailed procedures outlined in the methodology are used as a framework for implementation. Institutionalization addresses the coordination and procedures necessary to implement the solution defined by the EA. The methodology also provides procedures to help in the coordination of interface management as well as the identification of touch-points among organizations.

The institutionalization methodology describes how the EA should be used to implement the Army's logistics vision. The methodology defines a systematic approach to implementation where the proposed information flows across the enterprise. The institutionalization plan addresses the strategic methodology for configuration management of user needs once implemented. It includes the actual management processes used by Army Logistics to decide business process improvements, system configuration, and software changes. It designates those application domains necessary to plan for change and to maintain the SAP system.

The institutionalization methodology is aimed at the implementation and management of the business and the SAP system using commercial as opposed to developed products. The plan provides a systematic approach to product and organizational development that achieves a timely collaboration of relevant stakeholders throughout the SAP product life-cycle to satisfy customer needs.

3   General Solution Definition Approach

IDS Scheer, Inc and Enterprise Integration, Inc. (Eii) have defined standard software solutions for many large-scale and complex organizations. These organizations include the U.S. Army, the U.S. Navy, and many private sector organizations. In most of these consulting engagements, we are asked to provide an unbiased analysis of how standard software might align with the business processes of the implementing organization.

Standard software defines a class of information systems that are modular (e.g., Financials, Human Resources, Manufacturing, etc.) but, when implemented as a collection of modules, are integrated. These systems are not developed in-house but by commercial software providers (e.g., Oracle, PeopleSoft, SAP, etc.). Hence, the products are sometimes called "packaged software".

The implementing organization either accepts or rejects the business processes that can be enabled by the packaged software product. This implies that an analysis is required. The business processes in the packaged software must be compared with the target business processes in the receiving organization, and an accept/reject decision is required. That is to say, the business processes in the standard software are aligned with the business processes in the "to-be" Enterprise Architecture.

If the standard software solution is rejected, then the implementing organization searches for another product by a different provider, or custom-develops a system that precisely meets the requirements as documented in the Enterprise Architecture, or the packaged software is used as a baseline and custom development has to take place. If the standard software solution is accepted, then an implementation project is defined, and the software is implemented in accordance with an implementation methodology based on a Solution Architecture.

This section describes the high-level steps in a procedure that we have used with success. Our value-added contribution in this process is two-fold. Firstly, we have an automated toolset (i.e. the ARIS toolset) that supports our methodology. Secondly, we have business process representations of the major standard software products. There is much omitted detail in this overview as gap-fit analysis is a complex process, and this document is not intended to provide that detail. This section only defines one representation of the steps required to execute a gap-fit analysis. These are the steps in our gap-fit methodology.

1. Reviewing existing plans/vision. Standard software is aligned with the value-adding business processes of the implementing organization. Planning objectives define specific targets and time horizons for adding value. Hence, the business processes should be linked to the objectives in the organizational plan. If a plan does not exist, then one should be facilitated.

2. Developing initial scope and process ownership. Determining, as a first cut and at a high level, the business processes that will be included in the packaged

software implementation and the managers who are the decision-makers responsible with respect to those processes.

3. Reviewing performance measures and critical success factors. As mentioned in item 1, planning objectives are "linked" to functions in organizational business processes. The "link" between an objective and function is called a "performance measurement link." The target, as defined by the objective, is the success plateau. All performance measurement links should be documented and managed in a Solution Architecture.

4. Reviewing policies, procedures, regulations, and job descriptions. Policies, procedures, and regulations "bind" processes. Many are dated and obsolete. Many are self-imposed. The policies and procedures are revised in the light of the "leading practice" as presented in the standard software reference model or any model-based representation of the business processes that are executable by the software.

5. Documenting the as-is operational views, using an object-integrated methodology with a supporting automated toolset. Individuals and organizational units are responsible for executing functions that are embedded in cross-functional business processes. They are also responsible for meeting planning objectives. Hence, the operational model must be completely documented using a modern methodology and supporting toolset. This view is primarily of interest to managers, but at lower levels it is also used to document network topologies and other items of interest to technologists.

6. Documenting as-is function view using an object-integrated methodology with a supporting automated toolset. Function views are important to managers and technologists. The function tree is a hierarchical decomposition of the things that an organization does. While static, this view is essential to understanding the business processes that an integrated system has to support; i.e. if the functions in the organization are not supported by the executable functions in the information system, then a "gap" exists.

7. Documenting as-is business process view using an object-integrated methodology with a supporting automated toolset. This is the essential view for understanding cross-functional processes. This view documents the business processes. The business processes express the business rules of an organization.

8. Linking as-is organizational view. The object linking formally establishes function ownership. Since objectives are linked to functions, this link also formally establishes responsibility for meeting organizational objectives.

9. Developing as-is data view (at the cluster level) using an object-integrated methodology with a supporting automated toolset. This view describes, at the highest level, the sources and destinations of data that supports functions. This forms the basis for dataflow modeling, and given the nature of the problem, one may elect to construct dataflow models for the as-is situation.

10. Linking as-is data clusters. The data clusters are formally linked to the function objects. This documents, at the highest level, the data requirements. This will later allow the integration power of ERP packages to be demonstrated, since common legacy infrastructures are lacking on the data integration side. Data in the legacy world are distributed, redundant, and incomplete.

11. Creating should-be business process view. This procedure repeats steps five through nine for the business, as described in the policies and procedures manual. This step may be optional for some, but it is critical if one wishes to update the policies and procedures manual.

12. Documenting covert business processes using an object-integrated methodology with a supporting automated toolset. Covert processes are those workaround processes that are not officially sanctioned by management. While unofficial, they may be efficient; hence, they should be considered when revising business processes.

13. Documenting the target function view using an object-integrated methodology with a supporting automated toolset. This step documents the function view for the desired new way of doing business. This view is hypothetical in the sense that non-existent functions may be included. However, for packaged software, the target function view is typically a representation of the relevant functions supported by a standard software solution. For example, with mySAP, the target functions are typically selected from an SAP Solution Map. During an ERP evaluation not only a gap-fit exercise takes place. The future what-if analysis also plays an important role. If two ERP packages are a good fit for the current requirements, the possibilities of growth into new domains is a major factor for decisionmaking.

14. Documenting the target business process view using an object-integrated methodology with a supporting automated toolset. This step documents the business process view for the desired new way of doing business. This view is hypothetical in the sense that non-existent functions, events, and other objects may be included. It typically involves rearranging and organizing the target function view into business processes that address a particular policy, or an organizational strategic plan.

15. Documenting the target data view (at the cluster level) using an object-integrated methodology with a supporting automated toolset. This step documents the business data view for the desired new way of doing business. This view is hypothetical in the sense that non-existent data objects may be included. For packaged software, this step may not be required. If the relevant data is internal to the packaged software data model, it is usually not necessary to complete this step.

16. Linking target data clusters to target functions. This documents data sources and destinations at the highest level for the target architecture. This step is predicated on the relevance of the previous step. As mentioned under 10, this will show the power of integration.

17. Linking organizational plans to target architecture. This establishes targets, time horizons, and accountability for target business process execution. This is a crucial step, because functions that are not linked to objectives are candidates for outsourcing or elimination.

18. Aligning revised policies, procedures, and regulations with the target organizational views. The policies, procedures, and regulations must be revised so that they align with the new business processes. If policies, procedures, and regulations cannot be revised, then the target processes must be inefficiently constrained.

19. Documenting the reference architecture from the standard software solution using an object-integrated methodology with a supporting automated toolset. This step requires documenting the business processes, functions, data clusters, or other required views that are implied by the standard software. This is more difficult for some vendors than others. For example, SAP publishes its business processes whereas other vendors may not; hence, the business processes must be constructed. This may require a areverse-engineering of the standard software data models. Kirchmer (1999) is the reference for this procedure.

20. Performing gap analysis. Comparing the target views with the reference views from the standard software systems. Documenting and analyzing the differences. Unfortunately, there is no way to automate this process. It requires manual intervention and is usually executed by experts, or it is completed in small workshops that are comprised of software solution experts and domain subject matter experts.

21. Aligning standard software with business process. Documenting the software alignment with the target business processes. Analyzing the differences. Once again, this process cannot be automated. The gaps must be identified and documented in the solution architecture.

22. Accepting/rejecting standard software. If accepted, go to 20. If rejected, develop custom solution or best-of-breed solution (which could become a reference model).

23. Executing implementation procedural model. This is the detailed project management model in the form of an extended even-driven process chain model.

Rapid implementation procedures ignore the possibility that internal business processes may not agree with the processes implied by the standard software; i.e. an acceptable solution cannot be obtained by configuration alone. A rapid implementation may be achieved, but total costs are higher, since the standard software must be aligned with the business processes during the maintenance phase. Booker (2000) and the Boston Consulting Group (2000) address some of the problems associated with not completing the necessary up-front analysis prior to implementation.

4   Findings From the Architecture Study

Our standard approach had to be modified for the U.S. Army. In the case of the Army, a portion of the gap-fit methodology could be omitted, since the Army had pre-selected the SAP software solution. Hence, we focused on realizing the Army vision, given the constraint that the solution must be SAP. As previously noted, the Army enterprise vision is "A fully integrated knowledge environment that builds, sustains, and generates war-fighting capability through a fully integrated logistics enterprise based upon collaborative planning, knowledge management, and best-business practices."

To achieve this vision, the Army must be aligned so that the SAP software solution is optimized over "value chains," preserving the integration integrity of the product. This will enable the Army to maximize their support to the war-fighter customer with minimum investment dollars and resources. The business processes should be included inside the SAP solution boundaries without interfacing to leverage the benefits of integration. For the Army, the aligning of solution boundaries to preserve the integrity of the SAP software is a critical issue; i.e., costly Army-to-Army interfacing should be avoided whenever possible. For this reason, architectural planning is an absolute requirement.

We aligned the Army logistics enterprise with a single solution that is value chain-based and with fully integrated business processes. The primary integrating concept is Total Lifecycle Systems Management (TLCSM), as required by OSD guidance. In addition, other strategic directives such as End-to-End Customer Support and Condition-Based Maintenance (CBM) are also addressed in the architecture. The value chain view of the architecture is presented in figure 1.

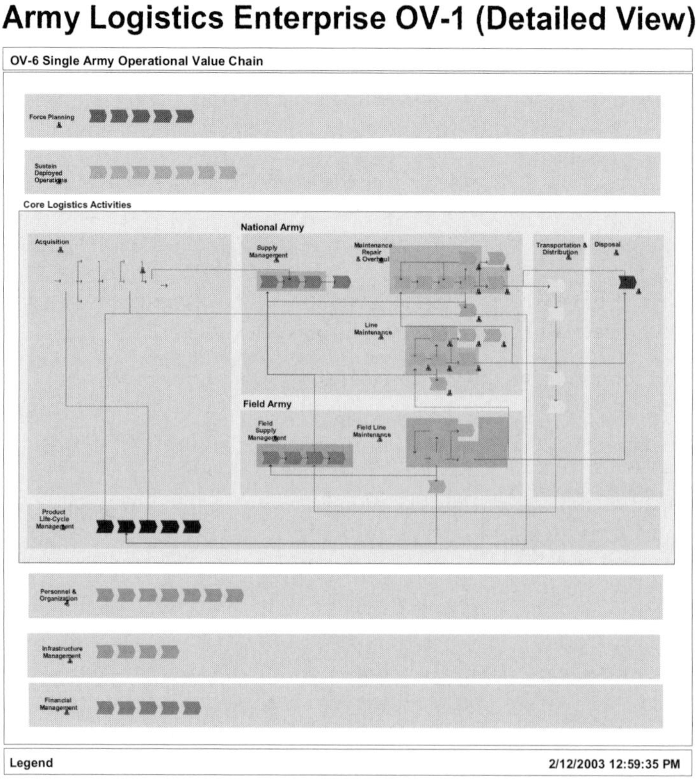

Army Logistics Enterprise OV-1 (Detailed View)

Fig. 1. Single Army Logistics Enterprise Architecture

Our major finding is that the business processes across the national and field Army are totally integrated, particularly in the area of product lifecycle management (i.e. technical data management, configuration management, document management, etc.). For example, technical data originates from a collaborative relationship that involves the weapon system program office and the Original Equipment Manufacture (OEM). This same technical data is used by the national Army to support sustainment operations, as well as the field Army while in garrison and deployed in theater. There is critical feedback at all levels of the technical data management process. This feedback begins at the platform level and flows to all levels of the organization, including a complete feedback to the OEM. Using the operational architecture created for the Army, we have demonstrated this requirement. The associated systems architecture that was produced has been structured to enable these types of critical business process requirements.

Given the level of complexity and degree of interdependence across the multiple levels within the Army, we have provided recommendations to address governance as a part of institutionalizing the single Army solution. Our experience shows that independently managed ERP projects lead to independent and disparate solutions. This conclusion is validated by Gartner research, and we addressed it in detail in the architecture study. The national and field Army solutions are very interdependent; therefore, independent configurations with independent contractor teams will not lead to an integrated solution for the Army. Our team demonstrated the dependencies and the complexities using the architecture.

A single Army focal point for SAP implementation management is required, and this single Army focal point needs a staff, a detailed build plan (i.e. architecture), and an enforcement mechanism. Since TLCSM is a core logistics function, the obvious focal point is the Office of the Deputy for Army Logistics Enterprise Integration (DALEI). However, as the team noted, this office needs funding to manage and coordinate all ERP and related EI implementations.

The team recommended that a Strategies, Architectures, and Standards Group (SASG) be established. The primary objectives of the SASG are to develop the on-going details of the architecture as well as maintain the integration build plan. The SASG reports to the Executive Steering Group (ESG), with oversight and management conducted by the DALEI. The team provided detailed recommendations on how the Office of the DALEI should maintain and manage the SASG, including how all system implementations must demonstrate architectural compliance prior to receiving permission to proceed through implementation methodology milestones.

The enforcement mechanism must come from the senior leadership, including the Commanding General of Army Materiel Command, and his personally selected Executive Committee in support of the DALEI. For logistics implementation projects, the guidance seems clear on these issues, and the team noted that central control was an absolute necessity. Our experience shows that successfully executing against the enterprise architecture is an extremely difficult and challenging task. There are many pitfalls that can derail even the "best-laid plans." Hence, architectural planning with a strong governance model is critical to success.

Assessments by the Gartner Group on Best Practices in ERP deployment and the associated cost/benefit data were also provided. Applying best practices can significantly improve the Army's ability to field a successful Logistics ERP program. The team addressed organizational critical success factors that consistently make or break an ERP architecture initiative. These factors include:

- The Right Governance Model,

- Organizational Change Management, and

- The Architecture Team Structure.

Suggested actions were placed with each recommendation to assist the Army as it addresses how to incorporate these best practices into its environment.

The Army's logistics applications and systems span enterprise boundaries, which mean that business process ownership is pivotal in facilitating collaboration within the Army and among other enterprise stakeholders. Collaboration requires integration, and integration requires a comprehensive understanding of business processes. A network of business process owners across the enterprise can provide input to the development of standard work processes and solution sets. This also allows innovative thinking and organizational differences to be captured at initial design rather than be treated as exceptions during implementation.

Additional findings and recommendations are listed below.

4.1 Additional Finding 1

The Army should avoid customization of their SAP solutions (or any packaged software for that matter). The Army should instead focus on reengineering its business processes to align with the software solutions and its embedded best-practice processes. This trade-off is cheaper in terms of avoiding software development costs, long-term support costs, and upgrade costs. In addition, a lack of customization will also enable the Army to drive its architectural design towards a single solution and in turn enhance its investment. This recommendation seems trivial, but it is directly related to our next finding.

4.2 Additional Finding 2

The Logistics Modernization Program began as a system replacement project for two legacy systems. Given the integrated nature of ERP software, this is an unusual scope for an SAP project; i.e. ERP is usually scoped to align with and maximize the value of business process domains. A similar approach is being taken for G-ARMY (i.e. replace 13 tactical systems). For both LMP and G-ARMY, some of the business processes are unique to national Army and the field Army respectively, and are not part of an overall Army and/or DoD business process.

However, some of the business processes from both projects are a part of a national (Army and DoD) business process domain. This makes the projects dependent on each other, other existing DoD systems, and all future system (SAP and other) implementation projects. There is a rare opportunity and a critical requirement to re-baseline the scope of the national and G-ARMY domains and pull all of the relevant business processes into the integration domain. This will help ensure that the Army maximizes its return on investment.

As a first step towards achieving end-to-end business process integration, the G-ARMY blueprint should be mapped to the business process architecture prior to entering the realization phase of the project. For G-ARMY, permission to proceed to the realization phase should depend on the ability to demonstrate how the blueprint enables the integrated value-chain architecture. Likewise, the details of the LMP scope [using an updated Business Process Master List (BPML)] should be mapped to the business process architecture prior to funding of any future SAP extensions. For the national level, all scope extensions should also be based on a clear demonstration that the effort extends value-chain integration. All integration-related contracts should be re-baselined to support this concept. Permission for scope extensions should also apply to all major non-SAP implementations.

4.3 Additional Finding 3

Product Lifecycle Management (PLM) is a critical Army business process. The team demonstrated that PLM is an end-to-end business process that flows across all levels of the Army, and it also interacts with the weapon system OEMs. In the Army today, the PLM process is disjointed and incomplete. In the architecture, the PLM business processes are completely integrated with those business processes that are enabled by SAP; hence, the PLM business processes must be managed as part of the overall Army integration effort.

The Army's ePDM effort should be realigned as an end-to-end business process implemented jointly with all other business processes in the Army integration domain. This implies that ePDM and ERP cannot proceed as independent projects. If the ePDM Program is allowed to proceed independently, technical data integration for the Army will not occur. On the management side, PDM implementation and all variants thereof should be managed by the Office of the DALEI in accordance with the architectural guidance of the SASG.

4.4 Additional Finding 4

The Enterprise Integrated Data Environment (EIDE) is an Enterprise Application Integration (EAI) entry point into the Defense Logistics Agency (DLA). The objective of the EIDE is to "provide an enhanced environment that enables the DoD Logistics Enterprise to execute practices, processes, applications and decision-support tools to achieve logistics interoperability and allow for information exchange within and between internal and external DoD business partners." The vision includes:

- "Non-system dependent transactions,

- Consolidation and reuse of interfaces,

- Data integration/sharing, and

- Leverage modernization efforts."

In the enterprise architecture we demonstrate that the Army is aligned with the vision of the EIDE.

5   Summary of Other Relevant Issues

Logistics chain efficiency comes from making good decisions based on accurate information. There is always an inherent tension between the cost of gathering the data and the measurable improvement in efficiency, operational needs, etc. The US DoD is moving toward CBM+ (as required by the Future Logistics Enterprise), with more accurate predictions of impending failures based on condition data.

Implementation should result in dramatic savings and improved weapon system availability to meet Combatant Commanders' requirements. CBM+ focuses on inserting technology into both new and legacy weapon systems that will support improved maintenance capabilities and business processes. It also involves integrating and changing business processes to improve logistics system responsiveness. Under consideration are capabilities such as enhanced prognosis/diagnosis techniques, failure trend analysis, electronic portable or point of maintenance aids, serial item management, automatic identification technology and data-driven interactive maintenance training.

The ultimate intent of this initiative is to increase operational availability and readiness throughout the weapon system life cycle at a reduced cost. Our team addressed several relevant integration scenarios. It appears that SAP can support these integrated scenarios. However, there are a number of issues that must be analyzed by the Army before the scenario can be implemented.

1. Industry and the Army must insert enhanced diagnostic and prognostic engineering capability into both new and legacy weapon systems to support improved logistics processes.

2. The Army must adopt the MIMOSA XML standard for the exchange of condition data between the weapon platform and business applications.

3. The Army must adopt the SAP Open Catalog Interface XML standard for interfacing the Interactive Electronic Technical Manual (IETM) parts catalog (part of the Repair Parts & Special Tool List) and SAP business applications.

4. The Army must develop an XML standard for the exchange of maintenance items between the IETM and the SAP business applications.

It is essential during deployments and exercises to be able to carry out the logistic and administrative core processes of an organizational element independently of the connection to a central SAP system. The fundamental requirements for detached and mobile operations can be expressed as:

- Modeling the personnel and material structures for the Army in the system.

- Supporting the Army's missions in all phases of deployment operations.

- Highly available IT functions that promote self sufficiency.

- Planning, building up, deploying and supporting Army contingents.

- Organizational flexibility.

- Integrated with the associated business processes, such as finance and human resources.

Our instructions in developing the architecture were to focus on technologies that will be mature in the 2006-2008 ranges, and not only on technologies that are mature today. The SAP mobile engine is not mature today, but it will be mature in the 2006-2008 ranges. Of course, the major benefit is that the SAP Mobile Engine is completely integrated with the Army Logistics Enterprise solution. It is not interfaced, and it is not platform-dependent. Our bias is always in the direction of integration as opposed to interfaced proprietary platform-specific devices, as long as business process requirements are met. We recommended that the Army engage the SAP development team to influence current development efforts and, through this process, ensure that U.S. Army requirements are met.

5.1 The SAP NetWeaver platform as an intelligent hub

The critical system architecture component for the ALE is an intelligent hub that manages data integration across multiple ERP solutions. We recommended that the hub be implemented using SAP technologies. More specifically, we suggested NetWeaver, Master Data Management, and SAP PLM, with SAP Exchange Infrastructure (XI) providing an optimal messaging engine across SAP domains and an Enterprise Application Integration (EAI) broker across external domains.

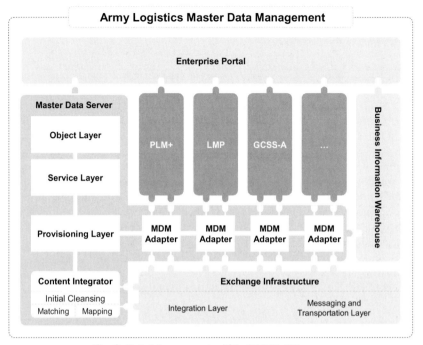

Fig. 2. Data Management within SAP NetWeaver

As a short summary, this alignment provides:

- Optimized messaging across all SAP domains, including G-Army and LMP;

- Master data harmonization and control at a single Army location,

- A single point for interfacing with all external constituents, including DFAS, DLA, and weapon system OEMs,

- Centralized repository management for all technical data, and

- Complete feedback to the OEM or any Army level for prognostic and diagnostic data.

We recommended that the combined NetWeaver, MDM, and PLM solution be implemented as a separately configured SAP solution. The recommended system architecture is presented in figure 3.

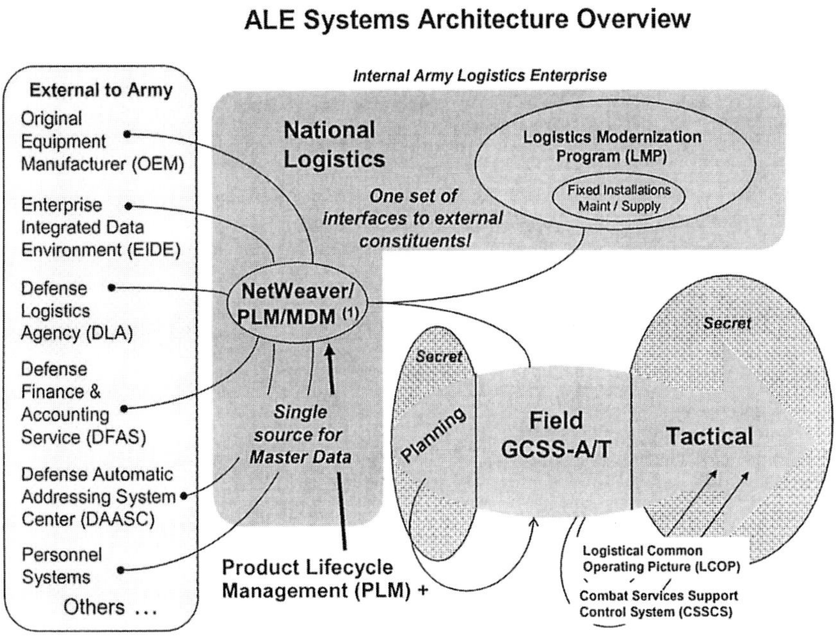

ALE Systems Architecture Overview

Fig. 3. SAP NetWeaver-Based Systems Architecture

6   References

Booker, Ellis, Enterprise Software Projects Rarely Satisfy, InternetWeek, March 28, 2000.

Getting Value from Enterprise Initiatives: A Survey of Executives, Boston Consulting Group, March 2000.

Kirchmer, Mathias, Business Process Oriented Implementation of Standard Software. New York: Springer-Verlag, 1999.

Scheer, A.-W. Architecture of Integrated Information Systems: Business Process Modeling. Berlin: Springer-Verlag, 1999a.

Scheer, A.-W. Architecture of Integrated Information Systems: Business Process Frameworks. Berlin: Springer-Verlag, 1999b.

U.S. Department of Defense, DOD Architectural Framework, Version 1.0, Volume I (Definitions and Guidelines) Washington, DC, 30 August 2003.

U.S. Department of Defense, DOD Architectural Framework, Version 1.0, Volume II (Product Descriptions) Washington, DC, 30 August 2003.

ARIS in Cross-Border E-Government - Integrated Automation of Public Services for the InfoCitizen

Otmar Adam
Institute for Information Systems (IWi) at the German Research Centre for Artificial Intelligence (DFKI)

Dirk Werth
Institute for Information Systems (IWi) at the German Research Centre for Artificial Intelligence (DFKI)

Fabrice Zangl
Institute for Information Systems (IWi) at the German Research Centre for Artificial Intelligence (DFKI)

Summary

The enlargement of the European Union will lead to higher cross-national mobility amongst European citizens. This will make public administration interaction across Europe more complicated. To ensure that this interaction does not become a barrier to citizens, European public administrations need to support E-Government in an information, communication and transaction stage, but above all in an integration stage. The interactions of processes from public services need to be integrated in an interoperable infrastructure. Such a solution was developed in the EU project "InfoCitizen" on a conceptual and technical level based on ARIS. The solution was proven to be working in a scenario simulating a real curriculum vitae of a mobile European citizen.

Key Words

Interoperability , Public Services , Information Architecture , Europe , Integration

1   Introduction

The European Union is constantly expanding. Thus, the number of cross-border curricula vitae will also grow. The mobility of European citizens will increase, as will their desire to work in other European countries. The European Union has committed itself to easing pan-European mobility.

As more European citizens seek to live or work across borders, and as more companies seek to settle in other European countries in an expanding European Union (EU), the greater the complexity of interaction between public services will become. Harmonization becomes harder with every new membership in the EU. This makes seamless interoperable integration necessary. Processes have to be integrated without the need to change their core.

A citizen born in a first country, living in a second country and getting married in a third encounters many administrative barriers. He has to deregister, register, provide a birth certificate or certify his civil status several times. Each time he has to go the public administration, he receives information on which documents to bring along, acquires the required documents, brings them back, uses the service (e.g. registration) and then might even have to pass on the information concerning the changes to other public administrations.

This not only involves time, resources and efforts for the citizen but might also be a reason not to cross a border within the EU. Hence, the complexity of public administrations currently represents a barrier to pan-European mobility. The consequence is that public services need to be integrated so that the European Union can truly expand.

2   Fourth-Stage E-Government

In the last two to three years, E-Government has received growing attention from politicians. E-Government is defined as the support of public service processes through the use of Information Technology (IT) [cf. Schmidt & Spoun 2001]. Many E-Government concepts are based on knowledge and experience acquired in the private sector with e-Business.

There are many avenues for public administrations to develop the provision of public services with IT and to exchange information and communicate with each other. Through the Internet, Extranets or Intranets, several forms of decision making, business processing or simple communication can change the way we interact with public administrations [cf. Schedler 2001].

E-Government alone will not revolutionize public administrations or the issues they face. However, E-Government might well be the tool that will enable public administration executives to drastically improve public services. Nevertheless, the degree of support for E-Government in public administrations strongly depends on the stage of realization.

To structure the degree of support in E-Government, the stage-wise realization model is often used [cf. Gisler & Spahni 2000]. It describes the realization through four stages that build on each other:

Information – This first stage is the easiest to implement. It describes electronic provision and availability of thematically structured and classified information. It represents a unidirectional communication relationship between public administrations and its customers.

Communication – The unidirectional communication relationship of the information stage is enriched by a feedback communication, hence a bi-directional communication between public administrations and their customers. Common technologies for this purpose are e-mail and forums.

Transaction – The transaction realization stage describes the online availability of public services. For instance, it becomes possible for a citizen to start a legally binding public service online. It can also include electronic payment and all relevant phases of a transaction

Integration – This last stage of realization is only rarely used (e.g. in [Gisler & Spahni 2000; Scheer et. al. 2003]). It describes the highest level of E-Government. It is the integration of the customer himself into the public administration processes as well as the integration of the public services. The customer can influence the execution of the public services without needing to know the way the public services work and process. It requires fully electronic support across all public services and their processes.

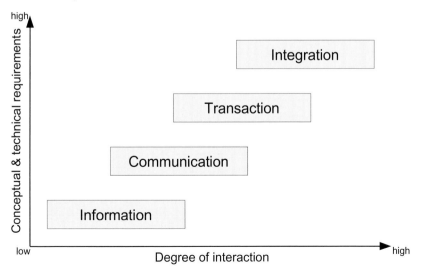

Fig. 1. Stage-Wise Realization Model

The stage-wise model describes not only the successive level of interaction but also the growing requirements in terms of security that need to be fulfilled for a specific stage. For example, the transaction stage calls for electronic authentication to ensure the identification and authenticity of a citizen. It also requires an electronic signature to guarantee and document the intention of public administrations' customers [cf. Bundesrat 2002].

3   European Public Service Integration

The support of E-Government in the information stage can already bring advantages. For instance, customers can see which documents are required to fulfill a transaction. Support in the transaction stage can improve provision of the service even further. However, under closer analysis one can see that it only offers a new distribution channel. The true potentials for improving service quality and reducing time and costs come with the integration of the public services. It gives a real added value to the public administration customers and can be classified into three categories [cf. Scheer et al. 1996]:

- *Process acceleration* – mainly through the reduction of transportation, processing and idle times

- *Process cost reduction* – mainly through lower resource and transportation costs

- *Process quality improvement* – mainly through the avoidance of errors as well as improved steering and controlling

The integration of public services allows the public services to be improved without changing the process structure. Nevertheless, looking at experience from the private sector, it is precisely the process restructuring, known as "Business Process Reengineering", that can improve the provision of services [cf. Scheer 1999, ARIS-Business Process Frameworks...].

Transferring this lesson to public administration implies that the transactional electronification of public service processes is only an instrument for providing services. Public services can only actually be improved by modifying and rationalizing the service provision processes, hence the way in which public services are offered. The best way to achieve this is to integrate processes. In general a process does not stand alone. It is connected in many ways with other processes. Analyzing and documenting the interacting relations makes it possible to define, adapt and optimize the process interfaces so that the processes can be integrated. The optimization of integrated processes brings the highest added value [cf. Mertens 2001].

In order to realize true pan-European public service integration, the processes need to be integrated without changing the local services and their frameworks themselves. Regulations and laws define the way services have to be provided. Only small changes in the process interfaces will enable the services to be integrated without the need to change the process itself. This is the only way to integrate services through the integration of processes in the medium term. This does not hinder future harmonization in public services and their processes in the long term.

Looking at the relation between single organizational units, such as departments of public administrations or whole public authorities, it becomes apparent that they are only integrated to a limited extent, if at all. However, a single standalone process (e.g. marriage) directly triggers several other processes (e.g. marriage certificate, civil status, etc.). Interaction between the public administrations takes place almost exclusively on paper using mail services or the citizen himself. It is not surprising that the consequence can be the loss of information and documents, especially those documents that are disadvantageous for the citizen. Apart from this effect, this form of interaction between services and processes implies loss of time and resources for the citizen.

The approach of integrated and transparent public services is to adapt the initiation of a process in such a manner that the customer only needs to request the service he/she directly needs, with all other related public services automatically triggered transparently.

- *Integrated* means that a public service process is capable of starting another related public service process needed to provide the public service initially required by the customer.

- *Transparent* means that a customer is freed of a public service process step which is not essential to him/her, making it no longer his/her duty to carry it out.

Public services related to an initial public service, be they preliminary or downstream in relation to it, can be characterized according the classic supply-demand scheme. A process requires information (demander) and another process can provide the required information (supplier). An initial service can be the supplier or demander accordingly:

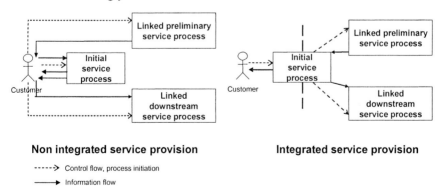

Fig. 2. Non-Integrated and Integrated Public Services

If an initial service acts as a demander, it requires information from other services. Since the knowledge of the required information only appears when the service is requested, the initial service has to dynamically request the information. Therefore, the service uses a pull strategy.

In the role of a supplier, the initial service has the potential to forward information. That information was created during the processing stage and can be forwarded to related downstream public service processes. As the downstream public services have no knowledge of the changes made by the initial service, it is up to the initial service to proactively deliver the information to the downstream services. This is called the push strategy [cf. Lienemann 2001].

While single-step transactions between customers and public administrations solely represent a new distribution channel, the integrated multi-step transactions that interact with other public administrations allow a drastic change in the overall process. Thus, they allow the provision of integrated and transparent public services.

In order to acquire the above-mentioned advantages of process integration, electronification is required. The information systems supporting the provision of the respective public services have to be networked electronically. How this can be achieved will be described in the sections below.

4   Realizing Cross-organizational Interoperability: The InfoCitizen Approach

4.1 The InfoCitizen Project

The project "InfoCitizen", funded by the European Commission under the 5th Research Framework Program, aims to create a pan-European Information Architecture for EPA (European Public Administrations) interoperability as well as to develop specific information technology that supports this architecture and ensures a seamless exchange of information between public administrations on a pan-European level. The specification and execution of interoperability was not limited to system integration but covered the whole lifecycle of interactions of organizations, public services, business processes and of course application systems. Moreover, with this solution EPAs were enabled to provide transparent and integrated public services for their citizens as well as for external clients.

The InfoCitizen approach involved analyzing several EPAs from different European countries and to retrieve common requirements for a transnational, cross-border solution. Based on these key criteria, an information architecture, namely the InfoCitizen European Architecture, was built, bringing about an effective and open solution to the conceptual and technical specification of seamless and pan-European E-Government interoperability, especially in terms of multi-agent settings and transparent service provision amongst EPAs. It was realized by implementing a set of generic software components, namely the InfoCitizen Software Framework that supports the ICEA, created by the use of leading-edge information technologies. This has significantly facilitated interaction, coordination and communication among EPAs, which was shown and proven with the deployment of a real-life-based demonstration scenario.

InfoCitizen started in September 2001 with a project volume of 3.3 million euros for a duration of 24 months. Eleven organizations in five EU-countries have worked together to take on the challenge of pan-European interoperability.

4.2 The InfoCitizen European Architecture

The first major outcome was the development of generic interoperability information architecture, the InfoCitizen European Architecture. It describes the relations and specifications of information exchange between EPAs, i.e. the inter-PA interaction. The major requirements addressed with this architecture are to support and describe the two key goals of the user's needs, i.e. [cf. Tarabanis et. al. 2001]:

- transparent public service provision to the European citizen,

- multi-agent/multi-country setting of public service provision.

4.2.1 Structure of the Architecture

The InfoCitizen European Architecture will conduct electronic transactions in multi-agent settings/multi-country settings in a transparent manner for the European citizen. For the implementation of an entirely new system with new requirements, the ARIS Life Cycle Model had to be broadened with additional phases. The ARIS Life Cycle was conceived as a procedural model for the implementation of software tools in business environments [cf. Scheer 1994]. Implementing a system without a top controlling structure to supervise and no kind of standard called for a new procedure. The design specification phase of the ARIS Life Cycle therefore had to be sub-divided into two additional phases. As a result, the specification phase is divided into the specification of three different architectures, each of them designed to solve a specific problem space on its level:

- *Conceptual architecture* – defining the business processes, information objects and the basic interoperability mechanisms by abstract models. To cover all different aspects that need to be described, it was necessary to use a set of different, originally incompatible modeling languages and methodologies and to adapt them both to satisfy the requirements of complete specifications and to convert them into a coherent overall methodology. The different description methodologies used came from ARIS, UML, AUML, FIPA and the SAP reference models.

- *Technical architecture* – this is a technology-independent description of the ICT; this description includes as few design decisions as possible and attempts to avoid any restrictions imposed by implementation technologies. The technical architecture follows the logic of the conceptual architecture in terms of service provision processes, service interaction and data structures. In other words, it is the "translation" of the business requirements from the EPA into a technical environment [cf. Carvalho et. al. 2003].

- *System architecture* – a description of the system "as-to-be-built" referring to its actual components as imposed by the selected technologies and incorporating design decisions regarding centralization/distribution, information representation formalisms, and other issues. The system architecture provides the guidelines for the implementation of the final prototype and imposes the technology to be used.

The procedure is described in the following figure:

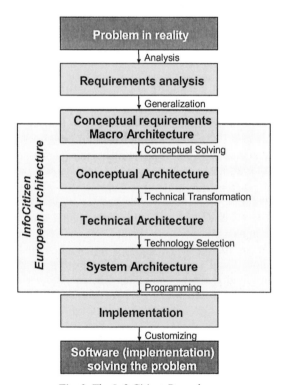

Fig. 3. The InfoCitizen Procedure

The main challenge of the European Architecture, especially of the Conceptual Architecture, was to control the knowledge for interaction and integration [cf. Adam et al. 2002]. The focal point in this context is the public service provided by a specific EPA. Both the inputs needed for processing the service as well as the outputs produced by the service have to be received respectively and distributed in a transparent manner to the citizen. To communicate successfully, the services must understand each other. In order to solve the confusion of data format mapping, the Common Document Language has been developed. This open and extensible specification describes the data to be exchanged within InfoCitizen. It relies on state-of-the-art XML technology and is based on existing standards. Using the Common Document Language, we provide a flexible instrument for finding a common definition of the syntax and semantics of data within EPAs without forcing them to change internally.

This solution makes it possible to integrate public services in an interoperable manner without the need to harmonize and thus without the need to standardize the processes of the EPAs.

In conclusion, the InfoCitizen European Architecture can be regarded as a new, innovative information architecture combining organizational aspects, views and requirements with ICT specifications and models that allow a generic but efficient description of E-Government interoperability at a macro and micro level, enabling the distributed InfoCitizen software solution.

4.2.2 Role of ARIS in the InfoCitizen European Architecture

The Architecture of Integrated Information Systems (ARIS) [cf. Scheer 1999, ARIS-Business Process Modeling...] aims to describe the structure and the behavior of enterprises and of their integrated business information systems. It includes the common method of business process modeling: the event-driven process chain (EPC). To enhance the compatibility of this approach to existing efforts for process documentation and management in EPAs, the InfoCitizen European Architecture was created in compliance with the ARIS methodology.

As already described, the main focus in this context is public service, which is provided by a specific business process. We therefore took a dualistic approach, defining the public service in an external view specified by its interfaces and in an internal view that defined its related business process.

Under the conceptual architecture, an InfoCitizen service in the external view is defined by:

1. *Preconditions* that have to be satisfied in order to initiate the process; e.g. only a man and a woman can initiate an 'intention to marry' service.

2. *Primary inputs,* i.e. input documents which are needed to initiate the service and that have to be provided by the initiator.

3. *Auxiliary inputs,* i.e. input documents that are needed in addition to the primary inputs in order to start the processing, i.e. the execution of the service, and that have to be provided not by the initiator but by third parties.

4. *Primary outputs,* i.e. requested output documents that are delivered, after the service execution, to the initiator/invoker of the service.

5. *Auxiliary output,* i.e. auxiliary output documents that are delivered, after the service execution, to third parties (especially other PAs), e.g. notifications or requests for updates.

The service definition and its interaction possibilities with other services are illustrated in the following collaboration diagram, figure 4:

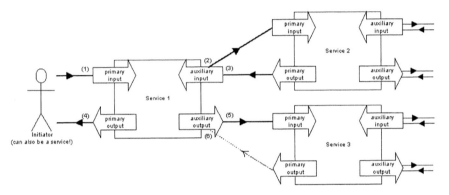

Fig. 4. Collaboration Diagram for InfoCitizen Services

Within the internal view, it is mandatory to describe the processing behavior of such a service. For this purpose, we link this service specification with a generic business process model that provides a template for the process logic of the public service. This permits representation of business cases in an adequate way without neglecting the subsequent IT-perspective.

The EPC of this ICEA generic process model is shown in figure 5:

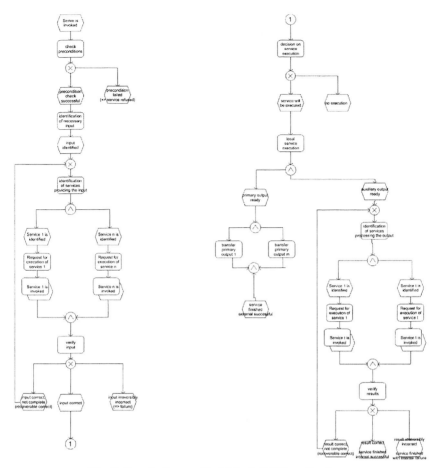

Fig. 5. Generic Process Model for InfoCitizen Services

The "structure" of the process is based on the fact that all PA processes considered for the application of the ICEA are citizen-triggered service processes. Something which all these services have in common is that the citizen has to formally apply for them. In other words, all of these service processes are decision processes. Starting from there, all processes can be abstracted by distinguishing different process phases that prepare or follow the actual decision.

The first step of an application process is always to examine the preconditions. If the process can generally be executed by an EPA (in terms of competence, availability etc.), the EPA has to check whether the necessary input for the execution of the process has been provided. Some input documents have to be provided by the citizen (ID documents etc.), whereas others may be obtainable by using the Info-Citizen public service network. If all input documents are correctly presented, the actual decision concerning the execution of the service has to be made on the basis of juridical conditions. Following positive notification, the service can be executed and the EPA provides the process results represented in documents that the EPA provides either directly to the citizen or to another EPA. The process description already takes into consideration the possibility of exchanging information or documents with other EPAs.

4.3 InfoCitizen Software Framework

The InfoCitizen Software Framework is a set of discrete software components that, together, make up the InfoCitizen software solution. This high dependency gave rise to the need for a coordination procedure to ensure that each component develops efficiently.

In order to guarantee wide adaptability and to avoid monolithic software con-structs, the project decided to develop an open framework mainly comprising four generic and fundamental software components linked via Web Service technology [cf. Fernández 2002].

The distinction of different component roles was introduced in the technology-independent technical architecture and was realized in a concrete setting in the system architecture. The main differentiation is made in central and distributed parts of the framework. The InfoCitizen framework consists of the Service Supply Components, each on top of a corresponding legacy system at a local installation, the unique Services Repository, the Interoperable Agent and finally the Front-End System. Figure 4 shows the structure of the InfoCitizen Software Framework.

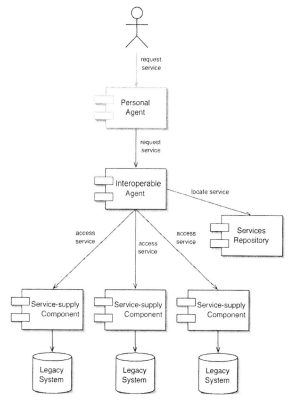

Fig. 6. InfoCitizen System Architecture

4.3.1. Service Supply Component Framework (SSCF)

The Service Supply Component Framework specifies how to develop components (Services Supply Components) that wrap PA systems and provide their services to the InfoCitizen Interoperability Platform. A Service Supply Component instance is a particular Web Service, compliant to the WSDL standard with SOAP1.1 binding on HTTP. A SSC can be developed with any programming language and deployed on any platform supporting the SOAP and WSDL standards. However, particular support is provided to develop Java-based SSCs.

An SSC Deployment Tool (SDT) is given to assist the administrator in all SSC lifetime operations – from their creation and customization to their deployment and installation.

Three generic and customizable SSCs are given both to exemplify the development of SSCs and to permit accessing a large number of common Executive Information Systems (EIS):

The *JDBC-SCC,* to allow a software agent (developed with Java, Visual Basic, C or any other language that supports SOAP) to access every JDBC-compliant database.

The *JCA-SCC,* to allow a software agent to access any software system compliant with the Java Connector Architecture (JCA) v. 2.0 through the so-called Common Client Interface. This standard has been specified by the Java Community to allow the EIS vendor to allow their products to be accessible from any J2EE-compliant platform.

The *CDL-SSC,* allowing access to PA documents stored in the legacy database through the Common Document Language defined by ICEA. This allows the definition of a mapping between the XML model of PA documents (described through the Common Document Language) and any relational schemas of a legacy database.

4.3.2 InfoCitizen Interoperability Platform (IIP)

The InfoCitizen Interoperability Platform (IIP, also referred to as ICIP) is the middleware that rests between the user Front-End and the Service Supply Components (SSC). It plans, controls and executes the information exchange. Using the emerging agent-technology enables the platform to efficiently search for, retrieve and distribute documents so that EPAs connected to the InfoCitizen platform can interact with each other, hence making them integrated. This is achieved by a combination of an Interoperable Agent and a Services Repository.

The core is an agent-based interoperability platform supporting distributed computing using the communicative capability of agents. It simplifies the implementation of multi-agent systems through a middleware. Communication between machines is supported by the use of standard SOAP. The agent platform can be distributed across machines, and the configuration, which can even be changed at run-time, is controlled via a remote general user interface. The platform comprises four main modules:

Interoperable Agent: The central element within the IIP. Its mission is to combine a set of atomic services provided by Service Supply Components into high-level operations performed as transactions. Can be accessed from the outside using both synchronous and asynchronous SOAP interfaces.

Services Repository: Database of InfoCitizen service description. Includes information for services, locations, extraction services, documents and document types. The service information was set up decentrally and updated by the EPA that is responsible for this specific service. When searching for an appropriate service, the Interoperability agent queries and analyses the data of the services repository and finally locates the specific service.

Repository Admin: Web front-end for repository data administration. Allows the usual operations for business object definitions: List, add, delete, and modify.

Extraction Service: Defines a mapping between data in two different documents. Is used to copy data back and forth from and between different inputs and outputs.

4.3.3 InfoCitizen Front-End System (IFES)

The Front-End System satisfies user needs for usability and process support. Based on internet technologies, it is a multi-lingual, customizable information portal solution that interfaces between the user and the InfoCitizen platform.

The primary objective of the Front-End System is to hide the underlying intricate infrastructure from the end user, who perceives it in a "black box" manner, while at the same time it cooperates seamlessly with the Interoperable Agent that runs the length and breadth of the whole distributed information system. Moreover, the Front-End System provides a different range of functionalities and options proportional to the rights of users of different categories.

Furthermore it is fully customizable in language terms and graphical representation morphology, so local, national platforms for the local public administration authorities can be installed and developed in an easy, friendly, fast and productive manner.

Although the Front-End System is comprised of many separate programs for the World Wide Environment (mainly CGI scripts), it retains a single unified look and feel. Hence, the end user perceives the whole system as a single web application and identifies the whole distributed system with the Front-End System.

The Front-End System of InfoCitizen comprises three discrete websites, each for a certain user level: PA employee, director and administrator. Each is suited to the corresponding user's access and user rights and presents him with relevant functionalities and an appropriate array of options.

4.3.4 InfoCitizen Common Document Language

The description of information exchanged through the InfoCitizen system is one of the most crucial aspects of the task of designing an interoperability architecture. As the information representation in the different EPAs is currently very heterogeneous, there is a need for standardized information exchange. All documents that might be exchanged by participating EPAs should follow a sort of common language understandable to the network peers.

The generic document concept used in the Dublin Core Model forms the ground concept for the Common Document Language. It structures the data and the metadata of all documents exchanged and sets the general rules for document exchange. On the technical level, it was necessary to define the syntax and the semantics of the common document language using a data dictionary in order to derive an XML-scheme for the system level specification.

The Common Document Language described within the technical architecture provides a technology-independent design for the generalized InfoCitizen document. This standardized language is an extendable basis for the handling of exchanged information between EPAs. To realize the standardization of the transferred data on the level of the system architecture, a technology has to be chosen that is widely accepted as a standard but at the same time is capable of dealing with the domain under consideration. XML can fulfill these requirements because on the one hand it is accepted and on the other hand it is extensible to comply with the specific needs of PAs.

5   Fielding Integrated Public Services: A Cross-Four-Countries Real-Life Demonstration

The InfoCitizen showcases will materialize the conceptual and architectural aspects of pan-European E-Government interoperability in order to verify the capabilities of the proposed solution. This pan-European demonstration was based on a complex and real-life scenario and covered four European municipalities and prefectures from Germany, Spain, Italy and Greece, in order to define, present and evaluate the essential interoperability that InfoCitizen Framework should provide to support A2A collaboration. The scenario has been constructed as a macro-process consisting of simpler processes. The basis for creating the scenario was to cover a large amount of cases and to verify and evaluate system interoperability. The final goal is for the scenario to lead to a pan-European Scenario taking cultural and legislative particularities of the EU countries into account so that the final framework can meet the real need of the PA organizations that will constitute the InfoCitizen PA organization network.

The deployment and customization of the generic components from the Software Framework enabled yielded practical experience using the InfoCitizen solution on real cases. The scenario has provided an appropriate test bed to check the viability of the InfoCitizen model with real PAs.

In brief, the pan-European scenario evolves the following PA organizations responsible for providing public services either directly for an EU citizen or for another EPA:

Municipality of Schmelz (Germany): In the whole scenario, Schmelz has to provide four different services. Schmelz will:

- Provide certificates of residence
- Deliver birth certificates
- Provide civil status certificates
- Certify citizens' German citizenship

A special problem was recognized during the detailed requirements analysis and afterwards in the showcase development. Birth certificates are kept as paper documents without a persistent electronic representation in Schmelz. Therefore, an asynchronous mode was introduced in InfoCitizen to handle partially or fully paper-based documents (offline-data-support).

Municipality of Tres Cantos (Spain): The demonstrator implements an interoperable census service. The service implies a workflow relating to the census process (registration/deregistration of a citizen in/from the census registry), which uses some other services offered by other municipalities, with the objective of requesting from the citizen as little paper documentation as possible and reducing to the maximum the citizens' presence in the administration.

Municipality of Colleferro (Italy): The Italian Showcase aims to apply the InfoCitizen platform to automate and integrate at a pan-European level some fundamental services provided by the Municipality of Colleferro to citizens:

- Change of residence from other countries to Colleferro

- Marriage in Colleferro between Italian and foreign people

Moreover, the Colleferro Municipality is not only involved in providing services for marriage and change of residence, but also in providing information required by services initiated by other PAs, for example issuing a citizen's birth certificate .

Prefecture of Thessaloniki (Greece): The Greek showcase is based on the adoption application process. The process for applying for an adoption is rather complex and consists of a large set of documents that can be issued from different PA organizations. InfoCitizen aims to facilitate this process that can be described conceptually as a set of steps which enable all the documents to be retrieved so that the PA employee has the necessary information to submit the application.

6   The Future of eEurope: Seamless, Pan-European E-Government Interoperability

Within a growing Europe and in spite of the huge efforts to counteract, heterogeneity within the European administrative space will increase rather than decrease. In order to face this development, the Union has either to make a significant cut forward to a unified legislative system or to introduce mechanisms and systems to deal with this diversity. The latter can only be achieved by holistic solutions that face the existing solution and realize efficient and effective organizational concepts and compliant ICT enabling electronic A2A transactions. One crucial step within this e-transformation of the Public Administrations is the introduction of business process modeling and management software. Thus the InfoCitizen conceptual and system architecture was created taking compatibility into account. The ARIS Toolset as a widely accepted standard tool for process modeling and optimization can export models into BPMI's Business Process Modeling Language (BPML). BPML is an XML-derived markup language and can be translated quite easily into any other XML-based language. The InfoCitizen repository uses such a language to store the information needed for business process automation. From a conceptual point of view, the Business Process models created in ARIS toolset can be exported and translated directly into the InfoCitizen repository and can thus be used immediately for cross-border business process automation.

Even if the first-level transaction support is not yet implemented in Europe, the InfoCitizen project already prepares the next step of full public administration integration. This is due to the concept of interoperable and integrated public administrations in the European InfoCitizen Architecture. Despite the heterogeneous environment, it is still possible to achieve organizational compatibility and comparability. Although integrated and transparent public services are only a milestone on the 'integration' level of E-Government, they nevertheless show the potentials and opportunities they entail. The open and extensible possibilities proposed by the InfoCitizen project to network public administrations on a pan-European level will reduce administrative borders in Europe. It will therefore allow the European citizen to feel a little more integrated and less limited in his life as a European.

In the long run, the InfoCitizen results are intended to serve as reference models for the electronic interaction of any public administration, thus establishing cost-effective and time-saving interoperability procedures that also improve the service quality vis-à-vis the citizen. Hence, enabling the public administrations in Europe to operatively provide transparent and integrated services on the local, regional, national and European levels means real "seamless, pan-European E-Government Interoperability". This is the challenge for the future. InfoCitizen is a first step towards this future.

7   References

Adam, O., Werth, D., Zangl, F.: Distributed Knowledge Repositories for Pan-European Public Services. In: Wimmer, M. (Ed.): Knowledge Management in Electronic Government, Springer, Berlin et al., 2002.

Bundesrat, Bericht über den Vote électronique: Chancen, Risiken und Machbarkeiten elektronischer Ausübung politischer Rechte, 9.1.2002.

Carvalho, J., Moreira, H., Sa-Soares, D.: An Architecture for European Public Administration Systems Interoperability. In: Proceedings of the 3rd European Conference on e-Government (ECEG 2003), Trinity College Dublin, Ireland, 3-4 July 2003.

Fernández, A.: Towards Interoperability amongst European Public Administrations. In: Lenk, K., Traunmüller, R. (Eds.): Electronic Government - First International Conference - EGOV 2002, Springer Publishing, Berlin et al., 2002.

Gisler, M.; Spahni, D.: E-Government – eine Standortbestimmung, Haupt Publishing, Bern, 2001.

Lienemann, C.: Informationslogistik, Symposium Publishing, Düsseldorf, 2001.

Mertens, P.: Integrierte Informationsverarbeitung 1 - Operative Systeme in der Industrie, 13th issue, Gabler Publishing, Wiesbaden, 2001.

Schedler, K.: eGovernment und neue Servicequalität der Verwaltung. In: Gisler, Michael; Spahni, Dieter (Eds.) eGovernment: eine Standortbestimmung, 2nd edition, Haupt Publishing, Bern et al., 2001.

Scheer, A.-W.: Business Process Engineering – Reference Models for Industrial Enterprises, Springer Publishing, Berlin, Heidelberg, 1994.

Scheer, A.-W.: ARIS-Business Process Frameworks: Frameworks, Springer Publishing, Berlin, Heidelberg, 1999.

Scheer, A.-W.: ARIS-Business Process Modeling, Springer Publishing, Berlin, Heidelberg, 1999.

Scheer, A.W., Kruppke, H., Heib, R.: E-Government – Prozessorientierung in der öffentlichen Verwaltung, Springer, Berlin, Heidelberg, 2003.

Scheer, A.-W.; Nüttgens, M.; Zimmermann, V.: Business Process Reengineering in der Verwaltung. In: Scheer, A.-W. (Ed.) Veröffentlichungen des Instituts für Wirtschaftsinformatik (IWi), Issue 129, Saarland University, Saarbrücken, 1996.

Schmidt, B.; Spoun, S.: Wege zum Electronic Government, IDT Working Paper No. 1, St. Gallen, 2001.

Tarabanis, K., Peristeras, V., Koumpis, A.: Towards a European Information Architecture for Public Administration: The InfoCITIZEN project. In: Stanford-Smith, B., Chiozza, E. (Eds.): E-work and E-commerce: Novel Solutions and Practices for a Global Networked Economy, Volume 2, IOS Press, Amsterdam, 2001.

Appendix: The Authors

Abolhassan, Dr. Ferri

Co-Chairman and CEO,
IDS Scheer AG

Altenkesseler Strasse 17
66115 Saarbrücken
Germany

Adam, Otmar

Lecturer,
Institute for Information Systems
(IWi) at the German Research Centre
for Artificial Intelligence (DFKI)

Stuhlsatzenhausweg 3
66123 Saarbrücken
Germany

Brady, Ed

IT Director,
American Meter Company

300 Welsh Road
Building One
Horsham, PA 19044-2234
USA

Cook, Yvonne

American Business Financial
Services, Inc

111 Presidential Blvd.
Bala Cynwyd, PA 19004
USA

Gahse, Frank

Senior Manager,
IDS Scheer AG

Altenkesseler Strasse 17
66115 Saarbrücken
Germany

Gulledge, Dr. Thomas R.

Professor and Director,
George Mason University

Enterprise Engineering Laboratory,
MS 2E4
Fairfax, VA 22030-4444
USA

Hadzipetros, Emmanuel

Senior Consultant,
IDS Scheer, Inc.

5555 Glenridge Connector
Suite 650
Atlanta, GA 30342
USA

Hafez, Wael

Senior Consultant,
IDS Scheer, Inc.

1205 Westlakes Drive, Suite 270
Berwyn, PA 19312
USA

Huntington, Greg

Director, Consulting,
Enterprise Integration, Inc.

11350 Random Hills Road, Suite 650
Fairfax, VA 22030
USA

Jost, Dr. Wolfram

Member of the Executive Board,
IDS Scheer AG

Altenkesseler Strasse 17
66115 Saarbrücken
Germany

Kirchmer, Dr. Mathias

President and CEO, IDS Scheer, Inc.

CEO, IDS Scheer Japan

Member of the Extended Executive Board, IDS Scheer AG

1205 Westlakes Drive
Berwyn, PA 19312
USA

Affiliated Faculty, Center for Organizational Dynamics, University of Pennsylvania

483 McNeil Building
3718 Locust Walk
Philadelphia, PA 19104-6286
USA

Lajmi, Rajiv

Consulting Services,
IDS Scheer SME Midatlantic

1055 Westlakes Drive
Berwyn, PA 19312
USA

Michaels, Jeff

President,
IDS Scheer SME Midatlantic

1055 Westlakes Drive
Berwyn, PA 19312
USA

Naidoo, Trevor

Director, Consulting Services,
IDS Scheer, Inc.

1055 Westlakes Drive Suite 100
Berwyn, PA 19312
USA

Scharsig, Marc

Managing Director,
IDS Scheer, Inc.

1205 Westlakes Drive,
Suite 100
Berwyn, PA 19312
USA

Scheer, Prof. Dr. Dr. hc. mult. August-Wilhelm

Founder and Chairman of the Supervisory Board, IDS Scheer AG

Altenkesseler Strasse 17
66115 Saarbrücken
Germany

Director, Institute of Information Systems (IWi), Universität des Saarlandes, Germany

Stuhlsatzenhausweg 3
66123 Saarbrücken
Germany

Scholz, Torsten

Product Marketing Manager,
IDS Scheer AG

Altenkesseler Straße 17
66115 Saarbrücken
Germany

Simon, Georg

Director, Consulting,
IDS Scheer, Inc.

1205 Westlakes Drive, Suite 270
Berwyn, PA 19312
USA

Steiner, PhD Donald

Chief Scientist,
WebV2, Inc.

510 Logue Ave
Mountain View, CA 94043
USA

Snyder, Chris

Consulting Services Manager,
IDS Scheer SME Midatlantic

1055 Westlakes Drive
Berwyn, PA 19312
USA

Wagner, Karl

Member of the Board of Management,
IDS Scheer AG

Altenkesseler Strasse 17
66115 Saarbrücken
Germany

Welchering, Björn

Marketing Consulting,
IDS Scheer AG

Altenkesseler Strasse 17
66115 Saarbrücken
Germany

Werth, Dirk

Project Coordinator,
Institute for Information Systems
(IWi) at the German Research Centre
for Artificial Intelligence (DFKI)

Stuhlsatzenhausweg 3
66123 Saarbrücken
Germany

Westermann, Peter

Senior Manager Cost-/Process-/
Quality Controlling,
DC Bank AG

Siemensstr. 7
70469 Stuttgart
Germany

Western, Colin

Vice President of Systems Planning,
a major Hollywood Motion Picture
Studio

Zangl, Fabrice

Researcher,
Institute for Information Systems
(IWi) at the German Research Centre
for Artificial Intelligence (DFKI)

Stuhlsatzenhausweg 3
66123 Saarbrücken
Germany

Druck: betz-druck GmbH, D-64291 Darmstadt
Verarbeitung: Buchbinderei Schaumann, D-64293 Darmstadt